NCS 기반

비즈니스 영문서 핸드북

Handbook of Business Documents

민선향
장은주
박경옥
하선영
유근선

도서출판 청람

■ 머리말 ■

최근 능력중심사회의 구현으로 대학에서의 교육은 직무를 기반으로 한 실무형 교육으로 전환되고 있다. 더욱이 글로벌 시대에 영어 의사소통능력은 모든 직무에서 요구되는 기초직업능력의 한 부분으로써 현장에서 활용할 수 있는 실용성이 더욱 요구된다.

이러한 변화에 맞추어 본 교재는 NCS(국가직무능력표준)를 기반으로 영문서 지원업무를 할 수 있도록 일반 사무직, 비서, 또는 관리자, 그리고 사무영어를 처음 접하는 학생들을 대상으로 교재를 전면 개편하였다. 그동안 학교에서 학생들이 처음 접하는 비즈니스 영문서라는 생소한 분야를 어떻게 쉽게 이해하여 현장으로 나가 업무능력과 연계시킬 수 있을지 실무 중심의 교재 개발 및 개편에 대한 고민을 계속하여 왔다. 특히 학생들의 영어수준, 그리고 산업체 현장수요, 그리고 비서나 일반사무 직무의 국가표준을 모두 반영하여 충족시키는 것은 쉽지 않은 작업이었다. 그동안 수많은 시행착오와 현직 종사자들의 피드백과 조언이 이 책의 귀중한 자료가 되었다.

본서는 총 3부분으로 영문서 숙달의 단계별로 구성하여 학생들 수준에 따라 사용할 수 있게 만들었다. 또한 모든 단계에 실제 상황을 바탕으로 수행예제를 제시하여 문제를 해결할 수 있도록 하였다. Part 1은 영문 비즈니스 문서를 처음 접하는 학생이나 직장인들을 대상으로 비즈니스 문서의 종류와 그에 따른 기본서식을 이해하고, 수신된 문서 종류 및 문서 내용을 파악하는 내용이다. Part 2는 영문서의 초안을 보고, 적합한 영문서 서식에 맞추어 워드를 활용하여 완성된 문서로 만들 수 있도록 실습과 병행하는 수행예제를 수록하였다. Part 3은 주어진 지시에 따라 문법과 형식에 맞추어 영문서를 작성할 수 있는 수준까지 연습할 수 있도록 구성하였다. 마지막으로 부록에는 영문 이력서 양식과 활용도가 높은 교과목명, 직함명 등을 정리하여 취업 준비에 도움을 주고자 하였다.

학교 현장에서 수십 년간 학생들을 가르쳐 온 5명의 저자들이 각자의 경험을 녹여 이 책에 담고자 했으나 아직도 독자들의 따끔한 질책과 조언이 필요하다. 이를 토대로 더 좋은 교재로 연구 보완할 것을 약속드린다. 끝으로 이 책이 나오기까지 애써 주신 도서출판 청람의 사장님과 편집 관계자분들, 그리고 자료 협조와 조언을 아끼지 않으신 현직 종사자분들, 감수자 ANP Asset 안애경 대표님께 다시 한번 감사를 드린다.

2017년 8월

저자 일동

차 례

PART 03

영문서 작성하기

[NCS 체계도]

[NCS-학습모듈의 위치]

대분류	경영・회계・사무
중분류	총무・인사
소분류	일반사무

세분류	능력단위	학습모듈명
비서	경영진 지원 업무	경영진 지원 업무
사무행정	경영환경 동향 분석	경영환경 동향 분석
	경영진 일정 관리	경영진 일정 관리
	출장 관리	출장 관리
	응대 업무	응대 업무
	보고 업무	보고 업무
	경영진 문서작성 관리	경영진 문서작성 관리
	회의의전 관리	회의의전 관리
	비서 사무정보 관리	비서 사무정보 관리
	경영진 예결산 관리	경영진 예결산 관리
	비서 영어회화업무	비서 영어회화업무
	영문서 지원 업무	**영문서 지원 업무**

[NCS 능력단위 요소 및 수행준거]

학습 모듈	NCS 수행준거	
	능력단위 요소 및 코드번호	수행준거
12. 영문서 지원 업무	1. 수신 영문서 내용 파악하기	1.1 영문 비즈니스 관련 용어를 수신 영문서 내용 파악에 활용할 수 있다.
		1.2 수신된 문서의 종류에 따라 수발신자를 파악할 수 있다.
		1.3 수신된 문서의 내용을 파악하여 관련자에게 보고할 수 있다.
	2. 영문서 작성 업무 지원하기	2.1 영문서 내용에 적합한 영문서 서식을 적용할 수 있다.
		2.2 상사가 필요로 하는 자료를 수집하여 제공할 수 있다.
		2.3 상사가 작성한 영문서의 초안을 서식에 맞추어 문서화할 수 있다.
	3. 비즈니스 영문서 작성하기	3.1 사용목적에 따른 영문서의 종류에 따라 필요한 구성요소와 형식을 파악할 수 있다.
		3.2 상사의 지시에 따라 정해진 시간 내에 문법과 형식에 맞추어 영문서를 작성할 수 있다.
		3.3 정확한 영문서 작성을 위해 초안을 검토하고 상사의 지시에 따라 수정・보완할 수 있다.

PART

01

수신 영문서 파악 및 보고

학습목표

- 영문 비즈니스 관련 용어를 수신 영문서 내용 파악에 활용할 수 있다.
- 수신된 문서의 종류에 따라 수·발신자를 파악할 수 있다.
- 수신된 문서의 내용을 파악하여 관련자에게 보고할 수 있다.

1 비즈니스 문서의 종류와 기본서식

(1) 비즈니스 레터(Business Letter)

❶ **CSC BUSINESS SOFTWARE** ← 레터헤드(Letterhead)

666 Fifth Avenue, Suite 1810, New York, NY 10036

Tel. 212-876-5432 Fax. 212-876-5433

www.cscsoftware.com

❷ March 17, 20-- ← 날짜(Date)

❸ Dr. Arne Grondahl ← 수신인 주소(Inside Address)

M&A Consultants

Anderson Co. Ltd.

556 East Philadelphia Avenue

Annapolis, Maryland 20899

❹ Dear Dr. Grondahl, ← 서두인사말(Greeting)

❺ Charles Lewis has asked me to confirm your luncheon meeting with him and a representative of Third Millennium at 12:30 on Friday, May 2.

본문(Body)

The Thai Monsoon Restaurant, located in the Metropolis Hotel at 29 West 49th Street, is close to numerous midtown offices, prime shopping districts, and you should have no trouble finding it. You will be Mr. Lewis's guest for lunch.

❻ Sincerely, ← 결구인사(Closing)

❼ *Jane Jones* ← 서명(Signature)

❽ Jane Jones ← 발신인 이름/직위 (Writer's identification)

Secretary to Mr. C. Lewis

❾ Enclosure ← 동봉물(Enclosure)

Exercise

다음 빈 칸에 비즈니스 레터의 구성요소를 적어보세요.

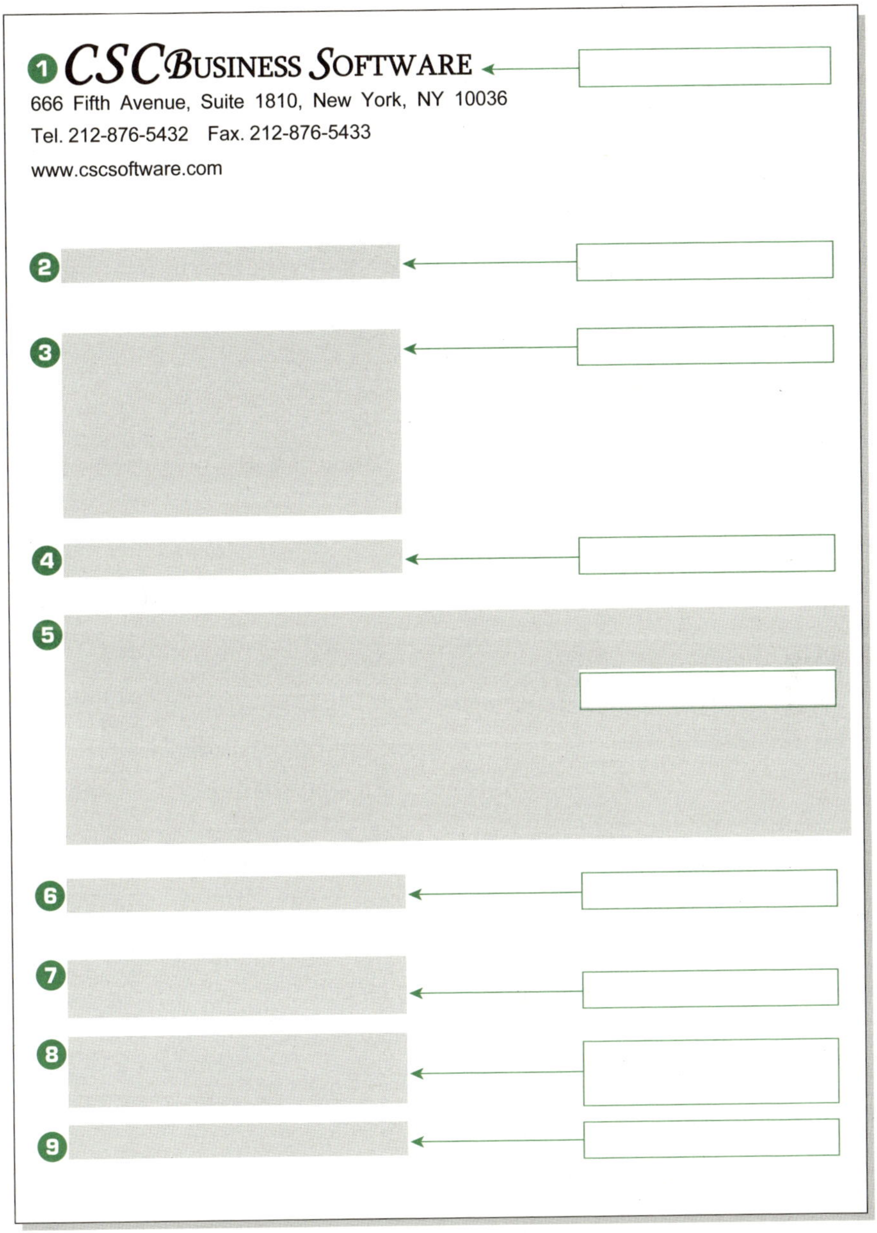

[요약: 비즈니스 레터의 구성요소]

레터헤드 – 발신자 정보(회사명, 주소, 전화번호, 팩스번호, 이메일 등)

수신인 이름/주소 – Mr. __________
직책
회사명
주소 1
주소 2
국가명

서두인사말 – Dear Mr. 000,

본문 – 문단 나눌 때 강제개행 금지

결구인사말 – Sincerely,

발신인 이름 – Soyoung Kim
직책

동봉물 – Enclosure

■ 봉투(Envelope)

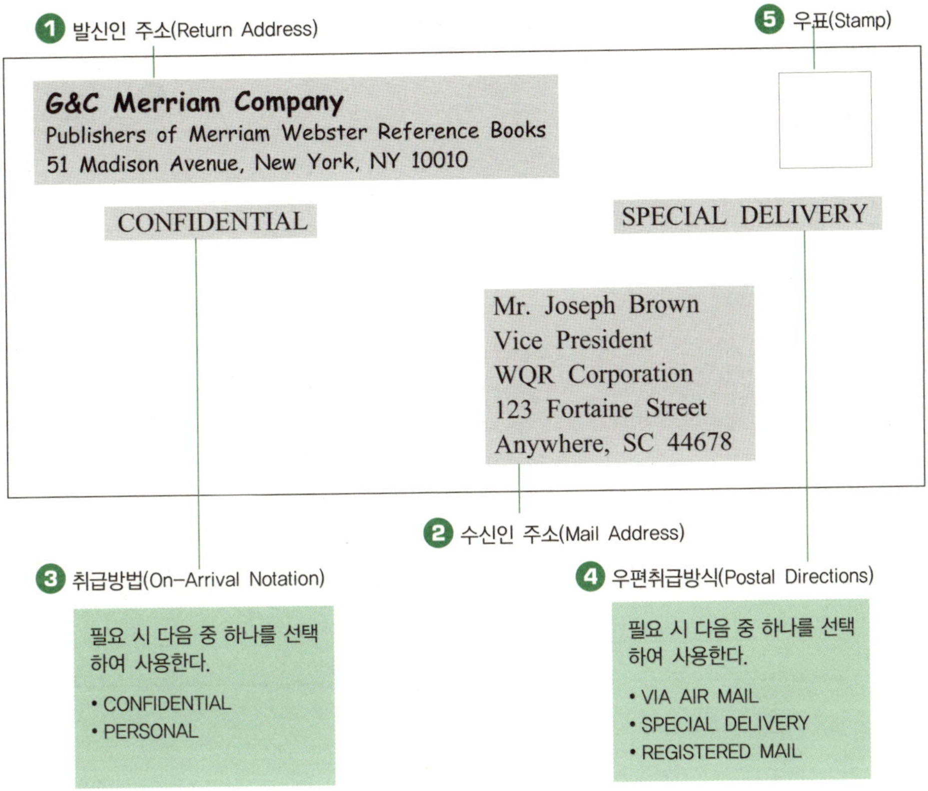

1 발신인 주소(Return Address)
5 우표(Stamp)
G&C Merriam Company
Publishers of Merriam Webster Reference Books
51 Madison Avenue, New York, NY 10010
CONFIDENTIAL
SPECIAL DELIVERY
Mr. Joseph Brown
Vice President
WQR Corporation
123 Fortaine Street
Anywhere, SC 44678
2 수신인 주소(Mail Address)
3 취급방법(On-Arrival Notation)
필요 시 다음 중 하나를 선택하여 사용한다.
• CONFIDENTIAL
• PERSONAL
4 우편취급방식(Postal Directions)
필요 시 다음 중 하나를 선택하여 사용한다.
• VIA AIR MAIL
• SPECIAL DELIVERY
• REGISTERED MAIL

Exercise

다음 빈 칸에 봉투의 구성요소를 적어보세요.

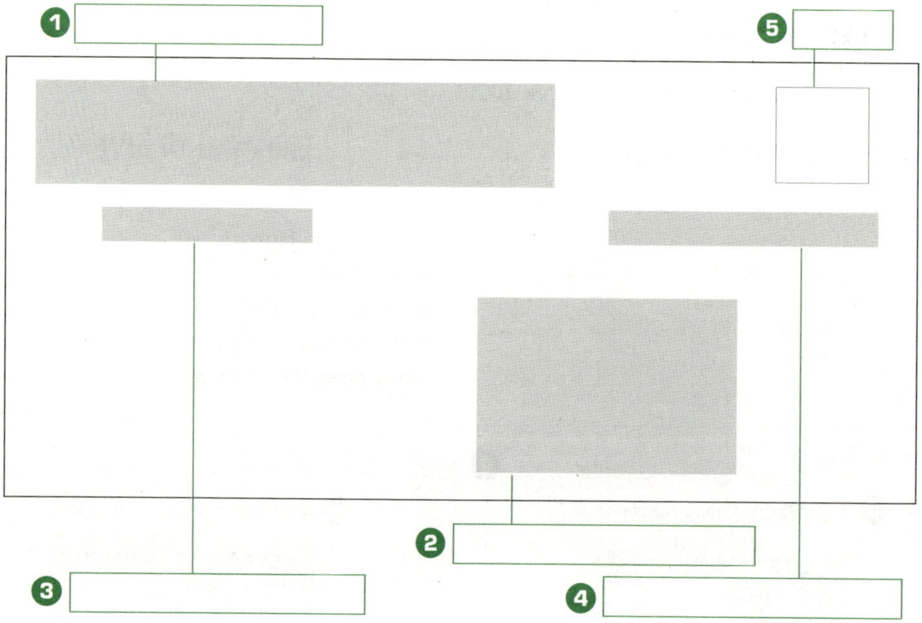

(2) 사내연락문(Memorandum)

Metro

Memorandum

TO : ← 수신자

FROM : ← 발신자 및 서명

DATE : ← 발신일

SUBJECT : ← 제목

An agenda is attached. You will also find a map with complete travel directions and a description of the parking facilities at the Tower Building.

↑ 본문

Exercise

다음 빈 칸에 메모의 구성요소를 적어보세요.

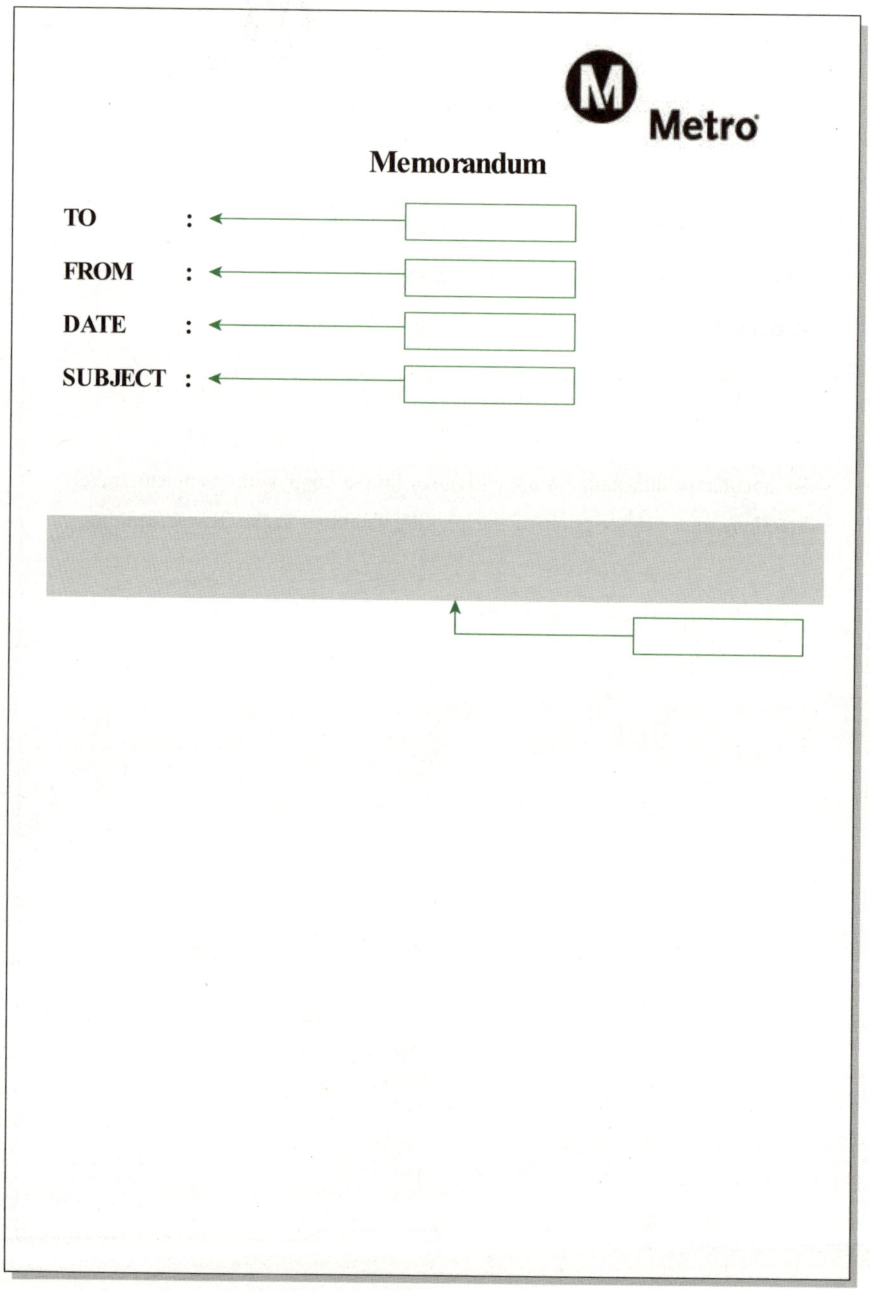

(3) 팩스(Fax)

FAX

Diners Plus
57 Stevenson Road
San Francisco, CA 97604
Phone.(415)665-0792 / Fax.(415)665-0716
e-mail. abc@diners.com
www.dinersplus.com

To:	팩스 수신인	**From:**	팩스 발신인
Telephone:	수신인 연락처	**Date:**	팩스 발송일
Fax:	수신인 팩스번호	**Pages:**	총 페이지 (including cover page)
Ref:	문서 참조번호	**Subject:**	문서 제목

This facsimile transmission is intended only for the use of the individual or entity to which it is addressed and may contain information which is privileged and confidential. If the reader of this message is not the intended recipient, or the employee responsible for delivering this communication is strictly prohibited. If you have received this communication in error, please immediately notify us by telephone to arrange for its return. Thank you.

팩스를 잘못 수신했을 경우 발송인에게 연락해 줄 것을 요청하는 서식 문구

Messages:

Dear Peter,

I am sorry that I was not in the office when you rang, but here is the information that you wanted. The address of our branch in Singapore is 54 Liu Fang Road, Jurong Town, Singapore 2262. The manager is Mr. S. Rushford.

John Blake

본문

Exercise

다음 빈 칸에 팩스의 구성요소의 이름을 적어보세요.

FAX

Diners Plus
57 Stevenson Road
San Francisco, CA 97604
Phone.(415)665-0792 / Fax.(415)665-0716
e-mail. abc@diners.com
www.dinersplus.com

To:	← [ ]	**From:**	← [ ]
Telephone:	← [ ]	**Date:**	← [ ]
Fax:	← [ ]	**Pages:**	← [ ]
Ref:	← [ ]	**Subject:**	← [ ]

This facsimile transmission is intended only for the use of the individual or entity to which it is addressed and may contain information which is privileged and confidential. If the reader of this message is not the intended recipient, or the employee responsible for delivering this communication is strictly prohibited. If you have received this communication in error, please immediately notify us by telephone to arrange for its return. Thank you.

↑ [ ]

Messages:

↑ [ ]

(4) 이메일(E-mail)

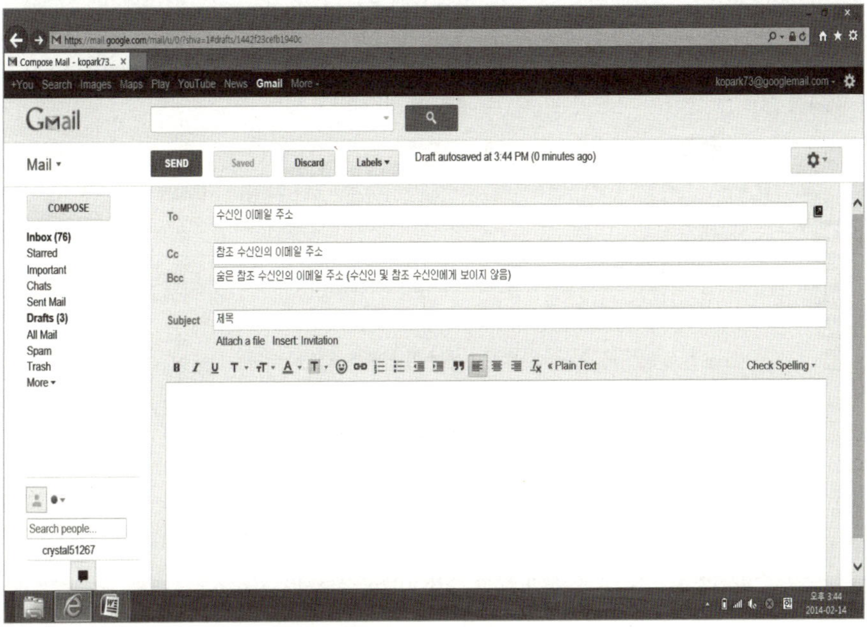
Compose Mail - kopark73...
+You Search Images Maps Play YouTube News Gmail More
kopark73@googlemail.com
Gmail
Mail
SEND
Saved
Discard
Labels
Draft autosaved at 3:44 PM (0 minutes ago)
COMPOSE
Inbox (76)
Starred
Important
Chats
Sent Mail
Drafts (3)
All Mail
Spam
Trash
More
To
수신인 이메일 주소
Cc
참조 수신인의 이메일 주소
Bcc
숨은 참조 수신인의 이메일 주소 (수신인 및 참조 수신인에게 보이지 않음)
Subject
제목
Attach a file Insert: Invitation
« Plain Text
Check Spelling
Search people...
crystal51267

Exercise

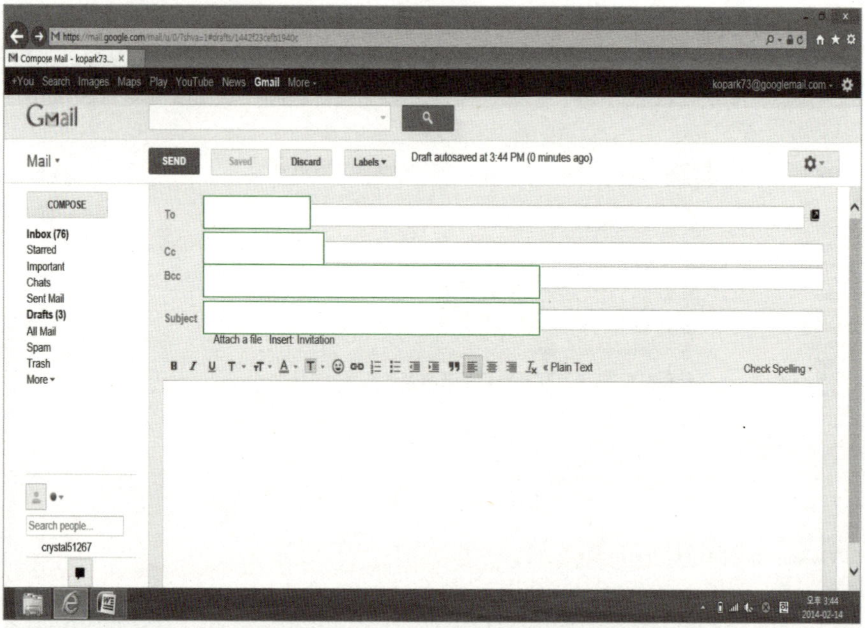
Compose Mail - kopark73...
+You Search Images Maps Play YouTube News Gmail More
kopark73@googlemail.com
Gmail
Mail
SEND
Saved
Discard
Labels
Draft autosaved at 3:44 PM (0 minutes ago)
COMPOSE
Inbox (76)
Starred
Important
Chats
Sent Mail
Drafts (3)
All Mail
Spam
Trash
More
To
Cc
Bcc
Subject
Attach a file Insert: Invitation
« Plain Text
Check Spelling
Search people...
crystal51267

2 비즈니스 문서 구성요소 이해

(1) 서두(Heading)

1) 인쇄서두(Letterhead)

Letterhead란 일반적으로 회사명, 로고(logo), 주소, 전화번호, 팩스번호, 이메일주소, 홈페이지 등을 명시한 것을 말한다. 즉, 발신자의 정보이다.

Merriam-Webster

Merriam-Webster Inc.

47 Federal Street•PO Box 281•Springfield MA 01102•Tel(413)734-3134•Fax (413)731-5979
www.merriam.com

2) 발신일자(Date)

- April 12, 20-- (미국식) – 미국식은 월, 일, 연도 순이며 일과 연도 사이에 콤마(,)를 찍는다.
- 12 April 20-- (영국식) – 영국식은 일, 월, 연도 순이며 사이에 콤마(,)를 찍지 않는다.

▶ **Name of the Month**	▶ **TIPS for the Date**
• 1월: January	• 1st: first
• 2월: February	• 2nd: second
• 3월: March	• 3rd: third
• 4월: April	• 4th: fourth
• 5월: May	• 5th: fifth
• 6월: June	• 6th: sixth
• 7월: July	• 7th: seventh
• 8월: August	• 8th: eighth
• 9월: September	• 9th: ninth
• 10월: October	• 10th: tenth
• 11월: November	• 12th: twelfth
• 12월: December	• 21st: twenty first
	• 22nd: twenty second
	• 23rd: twenty third

Exercise

다음 날짜를 비즈니스 문서 형식에 맞추어 영어로 적고 읽어보세요.

- 본인의 생일 ____________________
- 친구의 생일 ____________________
- 개교기념일 ____________________

3) 수신인 주소(Inside address)

수신인 이름, 수신인의 직책, 부서명, 회사명, 수신인의 주소 순으로 기입한다.

DIAMOND TRIUMPH AUTO GLASS

19-21 Jacquard Street, New Orleans, LA 70119

Tel : 504-969-6869 Fax : 504-964-7700

www.diamond.com

January 20, 20--

Mr. Joseph R. Rowe	수신인 이름(존칭, 이름, 성)
Manager	수신인 직책
Accounting Department	수신인 부서명
GWA Corporation	회사명(소속기관)
12 Smith Boulevard	수신인 주소 1(Address)
New York, NY 11010	수신인 주소 2(City, State Zip)
USA	수신인 주소 3(국가명)

Exercise

다음의 오른쪽 빈 칸에 수신자 주소의 구성요소를 적어보세요.

March 20, 20--

Dr. John C. Thomas ………………………… ____________

Associate Professor of Marketing ………………… ____________

Department of Business Administration ………… ____________

Santa Rosa State College ………………………… ____________

Santa Rosa, CA 95405 ………………………… ____________

USA ………………………………………… ____________

4) 서두인사말(Greeting)

서두인사말(Greeting)은 Dear 다음에 존칭과 이름을 쓴다. 이름을 쓸 때는 성과 이름을 동시에 쓰지 않으며 일반적으로는 성만 입력한 후, comma(,)나 colon(:)으로 마무리한다.

[서두인사말의 형식]

수신인	남자	여자
이름을 아는 경우	Dear Mr. ***,	Dear Ms. ***, Dear Mrs. ***, Dear Miss ***,
이름을 모르는 경우	Dear Sir or Madam, To whom it may concern: Hello Everybody,	

Dear Mr. Kim,

↑ 존칭 (Mr.) ↑ 성 (Kim)

Exercise

다음은 서두인사말이 틀리게 적혀있습니다. 빈 칸에 서두인사말을 올바르게 고치세요.

March 20, 20-- 발신일자

Mr. John C. Thomas ············ 수신인 이름
Associate Professor of Marketing ············ 수신인 직책
Department of Business Administration ············ 부서명
Santa Rosa State College ············ 회사명(학교)
Santa Rosa, CA 95405 ············ 수신인 주소

Dear Mr. John C. Thomas, ____________________ 서두인사말

(2) 본문(Body)

CSC BUSINESS SOFTWARE
666 Fifth Avenue, Suite 1810, New York, NY 10036
Tel. 212-876-5432 Fax. 212-876-5433

March 17, 20--

Dr. Arne Grondahl
M&A Consultants
Anderson Co. Ltd.
556 East Philadelphia Avenue
Annapolis, MD 20899

Dear Dr. Grondahl,

Charles Lewis has asked me to confirm your luncheon meeting with him and a representative of Third Millennium at 12:30 on Friday, May 2.

The Thai Monsoon Restaurant, located in the Metropolis Hotel at 29 West 49th Street, is close to numerous midtown offices, prime shopping districts, and you should have no trouble finding it. You will be Mr. Lewis's guest for lunch.

I am enclosing a map of the New York City area for your convenience.

문서 작성 Tip

- 같은 문단 내에서는 문장이 끝나더라도 엔터(Enter↵)를 넣지 않는다. 자동으로 넘어가게 한다(강제개행 금지).
- 문단과 문단 사이는 한 줄 띈다.

Exercise

다음 문장들을 문단작성 규칙에 따라 3문단으로 나누어 아래의 빈 칸에 적어 보세요.

Thank you for the Intertech Software catalog which you sent recently.
The programs look interesting and useful.
I am writing to ask if it is possible to receive a sample of the Astrowrite program.
Also, please send a price list for all the programs.
I look forward to hearing from you.

본문 위에 제목을 적을 수 있다. 제목의 형태는 아래와 같다.

RE: ______ 제목 ______

Regarding: ______ 제목 ______

Dear Mr. Reuter,

RE: Executive secretary position

Thank you for your letter. I am very much pleased to read that the executive secretarial position is mine.

(3) 결구(Closing)

1) 결구인사(Closing)

결구의 첫 글자는 반드시 대문자로 입력하고 comma(,)로 끝낸다.

Highly formal	Friendly & Less formal	Most friendly & informal
Respectfully yours, Respectfully, Very respectfully,	Sincerely yours, Yours sincerely, Sincerely,	Regards, Best regards, Best wishes,

2) 서명(Signature)

서명은 편지 발신인, 즉 작성자가 펜으로 직접 기입한다. 또는 서명 파일을 삽입할 수도 있다.

3) 발신인 이름/직위(Writer's Identification)

발신인 이름 앞에 존칭을 넣지 않는다. 발신인 이름과 직함, 부서명까지 기입할 수 있다.

Exercise

John D. Russel, Director, Consumer Products Division이 발송하는 편지의 결구인사말과 발신인 이름/직위/부서명을 적어보세요.

____________________ ← 결구인사말

____________________ ← 발신인 이름

____________________ ← 직위

____________________ ← 부서명

4) 동봉물(Enclosure)

서한문과 함께 동봉물이 있을 경우 반드시 서한문에 명시를 한다. 동봉물이 매우 중요한 것일 때는 동봉물의 내용을 명시해주는 것이 좋다.

동봉물 수	표현방법
한 장일 경우	Enclosure enc./encl.
두 장 이상일 경우	Enclosures Encs.
장 수를 명시할 경우	Enclosures(3) 3 encs. or Encs. 3
동봉물 수	표현방법
동봉물의 내용을 명시할 경우	Enclosures: (1) Annual Report (2017) 2 copies (2) List of Major Accounts (3) Profit and Loss Statement (2017)

3 수행실습

수행체계도

문서의 수·발신 정보를 확인한다.

↓

영문서 서식을 정한다.

↓

선택한 서식파일을 연다.

↓

문서의 초안을 작성한다.

↓

상사에게 보고하여 검토받는다.

↓

검토사항을 반영하여 수정·보완한다.

↓

상사의 결재를 받는다.

↓

수·발신 정보에 따라 발송한다.

수행 1 아래의 문서를 살펴보고 수행순서에 알맞게 상사에게 전달하세요.

MTA Express

988 North Crescent Rd.
Boston, MA 89700

May 30, 20--

Mr. Lawrence T. Reuter
CEO
Pro Agency Co.
370 Jay Street
Brooklyn, NY 11201

Dear Mr. Reuter,

Re: Acknowledgement of Receipt of a Contract
7
Thank you for returning the agreement so promptly. It came today with your letter and contract.

After the agreement has been recorded, a copy will be returned to you. The original along with the contract, will be kept by our attorney. He will return the contract to you at the termination of the agreement.

We appreciate your fine cooperation.

Sincerely yours,

Daehan Kim
Managing Director

출처: Anderson et al.(1970), The Administrative Secretary, p.302 재구성

[수행순서]

1. 발신인과 발신일자를 확인한다.

___

2. 수신인을 확인한다.

___

3. 사본 배부처를 확인한다.

___

4. 제목을 확인한다.

___

5. 내용을 파악한다.

___

___

___

___

6. 상사에게 보고한다.

사장님,
______로부터 ___가 왔습니다.
내용은 ______________
______________ 건입니다.

- 이메일로 전달할 수 있다.
- 프린트하여 중요한 부분을 표시하여 전달할 수 있다.

수행 2 아래의 문서를 살펴보고 수행순서에 알맞게 상사에게 전달하세요.

Memorandum

TO: All Salaried Employees

FROM: Lisa Vigil, Human Resources *Lisa*

DATE: June 2, 20--

SUBJECT: Health Care Benefit Plan

As of August 1, Middle Bass Island will contract with MedNet to begin a new health benefits program for all eligible salaried personnel. A brochure outlining important program information will be mailed to you soon.

If you have any queries regarding this new health benefit program, please call me at Ext. 1004. I will be happy to help you select the plan that is best for you.

[수행순서]

1. 발신인과 발신일자를 확인한다.

___

2. 수신인을 확인한다.

___

3. 사본 배부처를 확인한다.

___

4. 제목을 확인한다.

___

5. 내용을 파악한다.

___

___

___

___

6. 상사에게 보고한다.

사장님,

__________로부터 ____가 왔습니다.

내용은 ____________________

____________________ 건입니다.

수행 3 아래의 문서를 살펴보고 수행순서에 알맞게 상사에게 전달하세요.

FAX

Willoughby Hotel
812 Eastview Avenue
Brewster, NY 20897
Tel: (845) 520-0357
Fax: (845) 520-0350
reservation@willoughby.com
www.willoughby.com

To:	Mary Anderson Parker Mills	**From:**	Willoughby Hotel Reservation
Telephone:	(402) 241-7425	**Date:**	April 5, 20--
Fax:	(402) 241-7426	**Pages:**	2 (including cover page)
Ref:	PM43223	**Subject:**	Conference checklist

This facsimile transmission is intended only for the use of the individual or entity to which it is addressed and may contain information which is privileged andconfidential. If the reader of this message is not the intended recipient, or the employee responsible for delivering this communication is strictly prohibited. If you have received this communication in error, please immediately notify us by telephone to arrange for its return. Thank you.

Dear Mrs. Anderson:

Please find the attached checklist for conference rooms. Please let us know if there are any changes.

Sincerely,

Kay Stuart

Attachment

[수행순서]

1. 발신인과 발신일자를 확인한다.

2. 수신인을 확인한다.

3. 사본 배부처를 확인한다.

4. 제목을 확인한다.

5. 내용을 파악한다.

6. 상사에게 보고한다.

사장님,
______로부터 ____가 왔습니다.
내용은 ______________
______________ 건입니다.

수행 4 아래의 문서를 살펴보고 수행순서에 알맞게 상사에게 전달하세요.

To: Jihye Cha
cc:
Subject: Attachment Errors

Dear Jihye,

Thanks for e-mailing me the quotation, but the attached file does not properly open. Could you please resend it?

Regards.

Shinae Lim

[수행순서]

1. 발신인과 발신일자를 확인한다.

____

2. 수신인을 확인한다.

____

3. 사본 배부처를 확인한다.

____

4. 제목을 확인한다.

____

5. 내용을 파악한다.

____

____

____

____

6. 상사에게 보고한다.

사장님,
____________로부터 ____가 왔습니다.
내용은 ______________________________
______________________________ 건입니다.

PART

02

영문서 서식 활용

학습목표

- 영문서 내용에 적합한 영문서 서식을 적용할 수 있다.
- 상사가 필요로 하는 자료를 수집하여 제공할 수 있다.
- 상사가 작성한 영문서의 초안을 서식에 맞추어 문서화할 수 있다.

1 영문서 서식 스타일 이해 및 작성방법

(1) 비즈니스 레터(Business Letter)

1) Business Letter Styles(형태)

비즈니스 레터의 형태는 시대에 따라, 기업에 따라 다르다. 가장 중요한 것은 레터의 형식(layout)보다 일관성을 가지고 작성하는 것이다.

① Full-block Style

이 양식은 모든 부분의 좌측 여백을 수직으로 일정하게 남기는 양식으로 미국에서 많이 사용되는 형태이다.

CSC BUSINESS SOFTWARE
666 Fifth Avenue, Suite 1810, New York, NY 10036
Tel. 212-876-5432 Fax. 212-876-5433
www.cscsoftware.com

March 17, 20--

Dr. Arne Grondahl
M&A Consultants
Anderson Co. Ltd.
556 East Philadelphia Avenue
Annapolis, MD 20899

Dear Dr. Grondahl,

Charles Lewis has asked me to confirm your luncheon meeting with him and a representative of Third Millennium at 12:30 on Friday, May 2.

The Thai Monsoon Restaurant, located in the Metropolis Hotel at 29 West 49th Street, is convenient to numerous midtown offices and the prime shopping and entertainment districts, and you should have no trouble finding it. You will be Mr. Lewis's guest for lunch.

I am enclosing a map of the New York City area for your convenience.

Sincerely,

Jane Jones

Jane Jones

Enclosure

② Modified-block Style

이 양식은 모든 요소를 좌측에 수직으로 맞추는 것은 full-block 스타일과 동일하나 날짜(date)와 결구(closing), 서명(signature), 발신인명(writer's identification)은 편지의 중간에서 약간 오른쪽 부분에 기재한다.

CSC BUSINESS SOFTWARE

666 Fifth Avenue, Suite 1810 , New York, NY 10036
Tel. 212-876-5432 Fax. 212-876-5433
www.cscsoftware.com

March 17, 20--

Dr. Arne Grondahl
M&A Consultants
Anderson Co. Ltd.
556 East Philadelphia Avenue
Annapolis, MD 20899

Dear Dr. Grondahl,

Charles Lewis has asked me to confirm your luncheon meeting with him and a representative of Third Millennium at 12:30 on Friday, May 2.

The Thai Monsoon Restaurant, located in the Metropolis Hotel at 29 West 49th Street, is convenient to numerous midtown offices and the prime shopping and entertainment districts, and you should have no trouble finding it. You will be Mr. Lewis's guest for lunch.

I am enclosing a map of the New York City area for your convenience.

Sincerely,

Jane Jones

Jane Jones

Enclosure

2) 비즈니스 레터 작성방법

[비즈니스 레터(Business Letter) 매뉴얼]

Component Outsource Ltd.

119 South Barkay Bell, FL 32619
TEL: (407) 214-7788 / FAX: (407) 214-7789
www.component.com

↓ 1-5줄

날짜

↓ 1-3줄

수신인 이름
직책
수신인 주소 1
수신인 주소 2
수신인 주소 3

↓ 1줄

서두인사말

↓ 1줄

본문

↓ 1줄

결구인사

↓ 3줄

발신인 이름
발신인 직위
발신인 부서명

동봉물

문서 작성 Tip

- 여백: 페이지 레이아웃 → 여백 → 기본
- 글씨크기: pt 10 ~ 11
- 글꼴: Times New Roman, Arial, Verdana 등
- 한글 글꼴로 작성하지 않는다.
- 줄 간격: 전체 페이지의 2/3 이상이 되도록 줄간격을 설정한다.
- 본문의 문단 나누기: Block Style로 작성한다.
  즉, 한글문서처럼 한 글자(두 타) 들어가지 않고 처음부터 시작한다. 본문 중간에 엔터하지 않는다.
  문단을 나눌 때는 엔터를 두 번하여 문단과 문단 사이에 한 줄 삽입한다.

CSC BUSINESS SOFTWARE

666 Fifth Avenue, Suite 1810, New York, NY 10036
Tel. 212-876-5432 Fax. 212-876-5433
www.cscsoftware.com

March 17, 20--

Dr. Ame Grondahl
M&A Consultants
Anderson Co. Ltd.
556 East Philadelphia Avenue
Annapolis, MD 20899

Dear Dr. Grondahl,

Charles Lewis has asked me to confirm your luncheon meeting with him and a representative of Third Millennium at 12:30 on Friday, May 2.

The Thai Monsoon Restaurant, located in the Metropolis Hotel at 29 West 49th Street, is convenient to numerous midtown offices and the prime shopping and entertainment districts, and you should have no trouble finding it. You will be Mr. Lewis's guest for lunch.

I am enclosing a map of the New York City area for your convenience.

Sincerely,

Jane Jones

Jane Jones

Enclosure

Exercise

다음의 비즈니스 레터의 부분들을 살펴보고 다음 페이지의 빈칸에 순서에 맞게 표시해보세요.

THE BARCLAY

5500 South 96th Street, Omaha, NE 68127

Mr. Albert Durrell

Sincerely,

August 10, 20--

The letter will confirm your reservation for a single room for August 24-27. Your room will be available after 2 pm on the 24th.

C&C Company
2233 Connecticut Avenue
New York, NY 20008

Since you will be arriving in Omaha by plane, you may want to take advantage of the Barclay's Shuttle. Our limousine departs from the domestic terminal every half hour, and the service is free for guests of the hotel.

Enclosure

Dear Mr. Durrell,

Katie Grant
Director

(2) 사내연락문(Memorandum)

사내연락문(Memorandum 혹은 Memo)은 동일 조직 내의 사람들 사이에서 사용되므로 서신에 비해 형식을 덜 갖추는 경향이 있다. 비즈니스 레터와의 차이점은 Memo는 회사의 Letterhead 용지를 사용하지 않으며 수신인 주소, 서두인사말, 결구 등과 같은 격식을 차리는 부분은 많이 생략된다.

1) 수신인(To)

Memo를 받아볼 사람을 나타내며 일반적으로 Memo에서는 수신인 이름 앞에 존칭(Mr., Ms., Mrs.)은 상급자에게 존경을 나타낼 때만 사용된다. 직책, 부서명, 구내전화번호 등은 혼동을 피하기 위해서 포함되기도 한다.
여러 명이 사본을 받아보아야 할 경우에는 사본 송부처(cc notation)가 추가된다.

2) 발신인(From)

Memo를 보내는 사람을 나타내며 발신인 이름 앞에 존칭(Mr., Ms., Mrs.)은 붙이지 않는다. 그러나 직함이나 부서명 또는 구내전화번호는 정확성이나 편리성을 위해서 덧붙여질 수 있다.

3) 발신일자(Date)

Memo를 보내는 날짜로 서한문과 마찬가지로 미국식과 영국식 표현이 있다.

- April 12, 20-- (미국식)
- 12 April 20-- (영국식)

4) 제목(Subject)

제목은 본문의 내용이 무엇에 관한 것인지 간략하게 설명해주는 것으로 읽는 사람이 내용에 대해 준비를 할 수 있게 한다.

5) 본문(Body)

서한문과는 달리 형식적인 인사치레는 일반적으로 생략되며 다른 부분은 서한문과 유사하다.

대부분의 Memo 형태는 다음과 같다.

Memo의 일반 형태

Metro

Memorandum

TO:
FROM:
DATE:
SUBJECT:

문서 작성 Tip

- 본문은 서식에서 1~3줄 띄고 시작한다. 본문이 길어 여백이 없으면 1줄 띄고, 본문이 짧아 여백이 많으면 3줄까지 띄고 작성한다. 본문이 전체 페이지의 2/3 이상이 되는 것이 전체 모양이 보기 좋다.

다른 사항은 비즈니스 레터 작성 규정을 참조하세요.

- 여백: 페이지 레이아웃 → 여백 → 기본
- 글씨크기: pt 10 ~ 11
- 글꼴: Times New Roman, Arial, Verdana 등
- 한글 글꼴로 작성하지 않는다.
- 줄간격: 전체 페이지의 2/3 이상이 되도록 줄간격을 설정한다.
- 본문의 문단 나누기: Block Style로 작성한다.
  즉, 한글문서처럼 한 글자(두 타) 들어가지 않고 처음부터 시작한다. 본문 중간에 엔터하지 않는다.
  문단을 나눌 때는 엔터를 두 번하여 문단과 문단 사이에 한 줄 삽입한다.

Memorandum

TO: All Salaried Employees

FROM: Lisa Vigil, Human Resources *Lisa*

DATE: June 2, 20--

SUBJECT: Health Care Benefit Plan

As of August 1, Middle Bass Island will contract with MedNet to begin a new health benefits program for all eligible salaried personnel. A brochure outlining important program information will be mailed to you soon.

If you have any queries regarding this new health benefit program, please call me at Ext. 1004. I will be happy to help you select the plan that is best for you.

(3) 팩스(Fax)

1) 일자(Date)

날짜 표기법은 비즈니스 레터와 마찬가지로 미국식과 영국식이 있다.

- April 12, 20-- (미국식)
- 12 April 20-- (영국식)

2) 면 수(Number of pages)

표지(fax cover)와 함께 전송될 문서의 쪽수를 말한다. 팩스 표지를 포함한 총 페이지 수를 적는다 기입하는 방법은 아래와 같다.

- Pages: This only (total 1 page)
- Pages: This+2 (total 3 pages)
- Pages: Cover+4 (total 5 pages)
- Pages: 5 (total 5 pages)

Fax 전송 도중 문제가 발생하여 문서의 일부분이 전송되지 않을 경우를 대비해 반드시 총 페이지 수를 적어야 한다.

3) 수신인(To)

Fax를 받아볼 사람을 나타내며 성명, 회사명, 팩스번호가 기입된다. 수신인이 속한 조직이 대기업체일 경우는 정확성을 기하기 위해 직책, 부서명, 직통 전화・fax번호가 추가되기도 한다.

사본을 받아보아야 할 사람이 있을 경우에는 사본 송부처(cc notation)를 추가한다.

4) 발신인(From)

Fax를 발송하는 사람을 나타내며 발신인의 회사명이나 부서명, 전화번호 등이 겉표지(fax cover)에 인쇄되어 있을 경우는 생략하나, 그렇지 않을 경우는 덧붙여 넣어야 한다. 발신인 이름 옆에 발신인의 서명을 할 수 있다.

5) 제목(Subject)

본문의 내용을 유추할 수 있도록 간단히 적는다.

6) 참조(Reference)

문서의 참조번호를 기입하여 후에 다시 연락할 때 참고할 수 있다.

팩스 표지(Fax cover) 형태는 다음 그림과 같다.

팩스(Fax)의 매뉴얼

Fax

C&C Company
Jl. Barito II, No. 48, Kby Baru
Jakarata 11001, Indonesia
Phone: (021) 5200357
Fax: (021) 5493794
Email: info@shareware.com
www.cc.com

To:	팩스 수신인	**From:**	팩스 발신인
Telephone:	수신인 연락처	**Date:**	팩스 발송일
Fax:	수신인 팩스번호	**Pages:**	총 페이지 (including cover page)
Ref:	문서 참조번호	**Subject:**	문서 제목

This facsimile transmission is intended only for the use of the individual or entity to which it is addressed and may contain information which is privileged and confidential. If the reader of this message is not the intended recipient, or the employee responsible for delivering this communication is strictly prohibited. If you have received this communication in error, please immediately notify us by telephone to arrange for its return. Thank you.

Messages:

서두인사말

본문

결구인사말

서명

발신인 이름
직위

문서 작성 Tip

- 서식의 빈 칸을 모두 채워서 작성한다.
- 본문은 서식에서 1~3줄 띄고 시작한다. 본문이 길어 여백이 없으면 1줄 띄고, 본문이 짧아 여백이 많으면 3줄까지 띄고 작성한다. 본문이 전체 페이지의 2/3 이상이 되는 것이 전체 모양이 보기 좋다.

다른 사항은 비즈니스 레터 작성 규정을 참조하세요.

- 여백: 페이지 레이아웃 → 여백 → 기본
- 글씨크기: pt 10 ~ 11
- 글꼴: Times New Roman, Arial, Verdana 등
  한글 글꼴로 작성하지 않는다.
- 줄간격: 전체 페이지의 2/3 이상이 되도록 줄간격을 설정한다.
- 본문의 문단 나누기: Block Style로 작성한다.
  즉, 한글문서처럼 한 글자(두 타) 들어가지 않고 처음부터 시작한다. 본문 중간에 엔터 하지 않는다.
  문단을 나눌 때는 엔터를 두 번하여 문단과 문단 사이에 한 줄 삽입한다.

FAX

Willoughby Hotel
812 Eastview Avenue
Brewster, NY 20897
Tel: (845)5200357
Fax: (845) 520 0350
reservation@willoughby.com
www.willoughby.com

To:	Mary Anderson Parker Mills	From:	Willoughby Hotel Reservation
Telephone:	(402) 241-7425	Date:	April 5, 20--
Fax:	(402) 241-7426	Pages:	2 (including cover page)
Ref:	PM43223	Subject:	Conference checklist

This facsimile transmission is intended only for the use of the individual or entity to which it is addressed and may contain information which is privileged and confidential. If the reader of this message is not the intended recipient, or the employee responsible for delivering this communication is strictly prohibited. If you have received this communication in error, please immediately notify us by telephone to arrange for its return. Thank you.

Dear Mrs. Anderson:

Please find the attached checklist for conference rooms. Please let us know if you have any changes.

Sincerely,

Kay Stuart

Attachment

Exercise

다음의 팩스 부분들을 살펴보고 다음 페이지의 팩스 서식에 알맞게 표시해보세요.

Pages: This only (including cover page)

Date: June 15, 20--

Gregg Burke

Sincerely,

To: Koala Hotel
Reservations Department
Melbourne

Gregg Burke

We look forward to hearing from you.

Fax: (822) 355-7988

Dear Sir or Madam,

Re: Hotel information

From: Gregg Burke

Tel: (822) 355-7987

Ref: YK123

We would appreciate receiving information about your hotel's facilities including restaurants and meeting rooms as well as room charges. We also need to know about group rates and the travel agent's commission.

팩스(Fax)의 매뉴얼

Fax

C&C Company
Jl. Barito II, No. 48, Kby Baru
Jakarata 11001, Indonesia
Phone: (021) 5200357
Fax: (021) 5493794
Email: info@shareware.com
www.cc.com

To:	팩스 수신인	From:	팩스 발신인
Telephone:	수신인 연락처	Date:	팩스 발송일
Fax:	수신인 팩스번호	Pages:	총 페이지 (including cover page)
Ref:	문서 참조번호	Subject:	문서 제목

This facsimile transmission is intended only for the use of the individual or entity to which it is addressed and may contain information which is privileged and confidential. If the reader of this message is not the intended recipient, or the employee responsible for delivering this communication is strictly prohibited. If you have received this communication in error, please immediately notify us by telephone to arrange for its return. Thank you.

Messages:

서두인사말

본문

결구인사말

서명

발신인 이름
직위

(4) 이메일(E-mail)

필수요소	상대방이나 상황에 따른 부수적 요소
To(수신인) From(발신인) Date(발신일자) Subject(주제, 제목) Body(본문)	cc(사본 송부처) bcc(감추어진 사본 송부처) greeting(서두인사말) closing(결구) Writer's identification(발신인 이름 및 직위) Attachment(첨부서류)

1) 수신인(To)

상대방의 e-mail 주소를 입력한다.

2) 참조(CC)

함께 받는 사람을 말한다.

3) 숨은 참조(BCC)

Blind Carbon Copy의 약자로서 수신인 모르게 같은 내용을 제3자에게 보낼 경우 제3자의 e-mail 주소를 bcc 란에 쓴다. 그러면 To나 cc로 받는 수신인은 제3자, 즉 bcc로 받는 수신인이 있다는 것을 알지 못한다.

4) 발신인(From)

보내는 사람의 e-mail 주소를 쓰는 곳이다. 보통 소프트웨어를 작동한 시점에서는 자동으로 입력이 된다.

5) 발신일자(Date)

이메일 작성시간은 시스템에서 자동으로 입력된다. 수신시간은 수신자 밑에 나타난다.

6) 첨부(Attachment)

파일을 첨부한다. 본문에도 파일을 첨부함을 명시한다.

7) 제목(Subject)

E-mail에서 전체 내용을 간략하게 요약한 주제는 받는 사람이 받은 메시지 중 어느 것을 먼저 읽을 것인가를 결정하는 중요한 부분이므로 신경을 써야

할 부분이다.

제목은 약 25~35자 정도로 표시하며 막연한 제목(예: Reply, Information)보다는 내용을 짐작할 수 있는 것으로(예: Information on your catalogue) 써준다.

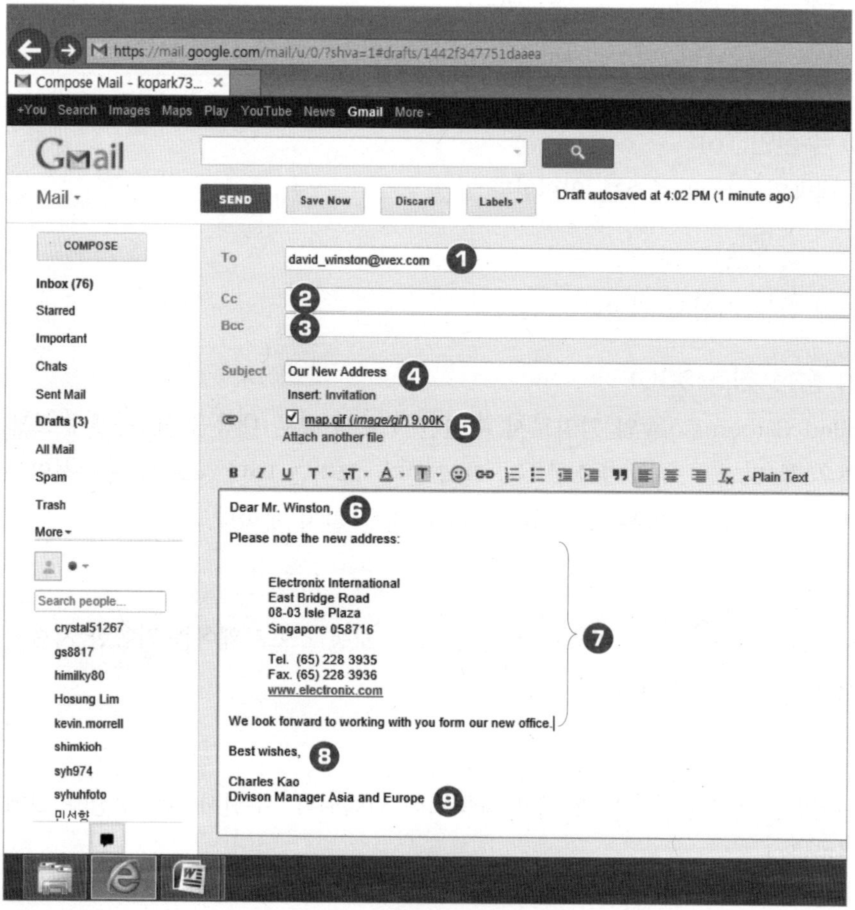

❶ To(수신인)
❷ cc(사본 송부처)
❸ bcc(감추어진 사본 송부처)
❹ Subject(주제)
❺ Attachment File(첨부파일)
❻ greeting(서두인사)
❼ Body(본문)
❽ closing(결구인사)
❾ Writer's Identification(발신인 이름 및 직위)

문서 작성 Tip

- 답장을 작성할 때는 [답장] 버튼을 클릭하여 수신한 이메일의 윗부분에 작성한다.
- 답장은 다른 색 글씨로 작성하면 구분하기가 좋다.
- 답장할 내용이 많을 때는 수신한 문서의 해당 부분에 다른 색 글씨로 작성할 수도 있다.

다른 사항은 비즈니스 레터 작성 규정을 참조하세요.

- 글씨크기: pt 10 ~ 11
- 글꼴: Times New Roman, Arial, Verdana 등
  한글 글꼴로 작성하지 않는다.
- 본문의 문단 나누기: Block Style로 작성한다.
  즉, 한글문서처럼 한 글자(두 타) 들어가지 않고 처음부터 시작한다. 본문 중간에 엔터하지 않는다.
  문단을 나눌 때는 엔터를 두 번하여 문단과 문단 사이에 한 줄 삽입한다.

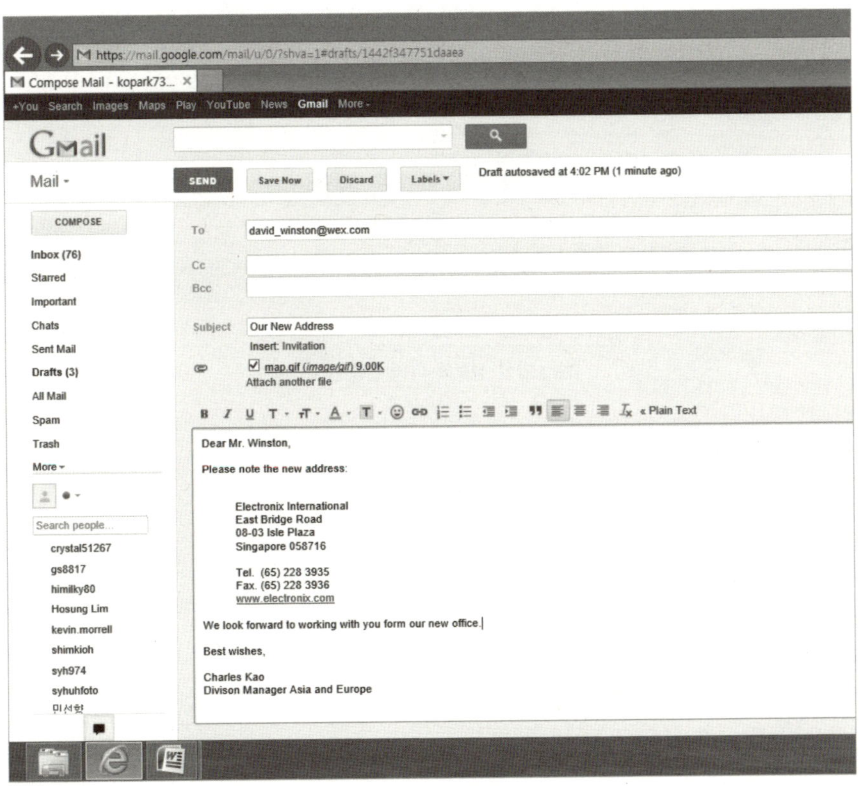

2 수행실습

수행체계도

문서의 수·발신 정보를 확인한다.

↓

영문서 서식을 정한다.

↓

선택한 서식파일을 연다.

↓

문서의 초안을 작성한다.

↓

상사에게 보고하여 검토받는다.

↓

검토사항을 반영하여 수정·보완한다.

↓

상사의 결재를 받는다.

↓

수·발신 정보에 따라 발송한다.

수행 1

김미영 비서는 아래의 문서를 수신하였다. 이에 대한 회신 문서를 작성하라는 상사의 메모를 받았다. 아래의 내용을 토대로 완성된 형태의 문서를 작성하세요.

To: Jihye Cha
cc:
Subject: Attachment Errors

Dear Jihye,

Thanks for e-mailing me the quotation, but the attached file does not properly open. Could you please resend it?

Regards.

Shinae Lim

김미영 씨,
메모의 내용으로
답신을 발송하고 파일
다시 보내주세요.

I am resending the file. Please feel free to contact me if you have any problems. Thanks.

- **quotation**: 견적
- **attached file**: 첨부파일

[수행순서]

반 ___ 학번 ________ 이름 ________ 제출일 ________

다음 수행순서에 알맞게 문서가 작성되었는지 살펴보고 확인 칸에 체크표시하세요.

번호	수행순서	확인
1	문서의 종류를 정한다.	☐
2	서식파일을 연다.	☐
3	문서를 작성한다.	☐
4	초안을 검토한다.	☐
5	상사에게 보고한다.	☐
6	발신인과 발신정보를 확인하여 발송한다.	☐

보고 Tip:

사장님,

__________씨에게 발송할 _____의 초안을 작성하였습니다.

내용은 ______________________________

____________________ 건입니다.

검토하시고 수정할 사항이 있으시면 말씀하여 주십시오.

[작성 결과물 체크리스트]

	내용	Yes	No
1	답장의 위치가 적절한가?	☐	☐
2	오탈자를 확인하였는가?	☐	☐
3	본문의 문단 나누기가 적절한가?	☐	☐
4	문서 양식에 따른 구성요소가 모두 포함되었는가?	☐	☐
5	첨부파일이 있는지 확인하였는가?	☐	☐

수행 2

상사가 아래의 내용과 같이 문서를 발신하라고 지시하였다. 아래의 내용을 토대로 완성된 형태의 문서를 작성하세요.

날짜: 오늘 날짜

수신인: All employees, MESA Sports Supplies Ltd.

발신인: Vincent Ohly, Human Resources Manager, MESA Sports Supplies Ltd.

제목: 제목 삽입

내용:
Following the successful launch of the computer training department last year, we now plan to offer a range of new computer courses to all employees. Please discuss your training requirements with your manager by June 1 and enroll for a course by June 10.

- **launch**: (새로운 사업의)개시, (배의)진수
- **offer**: 제공하다
- **range**: 범위, 폭
- **employee**: 종업원, 직원
- **training**: 훈련
- **requirement**: 필요조건, 자격, 요건
- **enroll**: 등록하다

[수행순서]

반 ____ 학번 __________ 이름 __________ 제출일 __________

다음 수행순서에 알맞게 문서가 작성되었는지 살펴보고 확인 칸에 체크표시하세요.

번호	수행순서	확인
1	문서의 종류를 정한다.	☐
2	서식파일을 연다.	☐
3	문서를 작성한다.	☐
4	초안을 검토한다.	☐
5	상사에게 보고한다.	☐
6	발신인과 발신 정보를 확인하여 발송한다.	☐

보고 Tip:

사장님,
____________씨에게 발송할 ______의 초안을 작성하였습니다.
내용은 ________________________________
________________________ 건입니다.
검토하시고 수정할 사항이 있으시면 말씀하여 주십시오.

[작성 결과물 체크리스트]

	내용	Yes	No
1	문서 양식에 따른 구성요소가 모두 포함되었는가?	☐	☐
2	본문의 문단 나누기가 적절한가?	☐	☐
3	문서의 전체적 레이아웃이 적절한가? (여백)	☐	☐
4	문서의 모양이 적절한가? (글씨체, 글씨크기, 줄간격 등)	☐	☐
5	오탈자를 확인하였는가?	☐	☐

수행 3

김미영 비서는 아래의 내용으로 문서를 발송하라는 상사의 지시를 받았다. 적절한 문서 서식을 선택하여 오탈자 등을 수정한 형식에 맞는 형태로 작성해보세요.

Wilson & Company Ltd.
51 Wilbleton Road
Toronto, ON M6K 3C3, Canada
Tel (416) 889-2356 Fax (416) 889-3489
www.wilson.com

May 5, 20--

SUPPLIES LIMITED
316 wilson boulevard
Arlington, VA 22207
usa

sir or Dear madam,

this morning I received a carton of computer printout paper (stock number CP4-9. The paper is useless - the carton was damaged and wet, I'm returning it under separate cover

We'd like a replacement as soon as possible

please call me if there are any questions? thank you for your cooperation.

cordially yours

Sophie Yang

[수행순서]

반 ___ 학번 ________ 이름 ________ 제출일 ________

다음 수행순서에 알맞게 문서가 작성되었는지 살펴보고 확인 칸에 체크표시하세요.

번호	수행순서	확인
1	문서의 종류를 정한다.	☐
2	서식파일을 연다.	☐
3	문서를 작성한다.	☐
4	초안을 검토한다.	☐
5	상사에게 보고한다.	☐
6	발신인과 발신정보를 확인하여 발송한다.	☐

보고 Tip:

사장님,

__________씨에게 발송할 _____의 초안을 작성하였습니다.

내용은 ______________________________

______________________ 건입니다.

검토하시고 수정할 사항이 있으시면 말씀하여 주십시오.

[작성 결과물 체크리스트]

	내용	Yes	No
1	문서 양식에 따른 구성요소가 모두 포함되었는가?	☐	☐
2	본문의 문단 나누기가 적절한가?	☐	☐
3	문서의 전체적 레이아웃이 적절한가? (여백)	☐	☐
4	문서의 모양이 적절한가? (글씨체, 글씨크기, 줄간격 등)	☐	☐
5	오탈자를 확인하였는가?	☐	☐

수행 4

상사가 아래의 내용과 같이 문서를 발신하라고 지시하였다. 아래의 사항을 토대로 완성된 문서로 작성하세요.

날짜: 오늘 날짜

수신인: The Production Supervisor, Leefung Plastics (Singapore) Ltd., PO Box 226, Brown Street, Singapore
Tel: (+63) 561-2287 Fax (+63) 561-2290

발신인: Jun Mizuno
International Relations Section, Leefung Plastics Ltd., **56 Hennessy Road Hong Kong**
Tel: (+852) 348 172 Fax (+852) 348 296

제목: 제목 삽입

I am writing in connection with the General Manager's Forthcoming trip to South East Asia.

The GM will visit Singapore on 9-10 March. While she is there, she would like to speak to all members of the Production Dept. Please could you cancel all appointments for these days? I'll attach her appointment schedule list.

Attachment

영문 출장일정표

ITINERARY

Mr. Michael Laurence | **January 10-13, 2015**

Monday, January 10 (Seoul to New York City)	
10:00 am	Leave Seoul Incheon Int'l Airport on Korean Air Flight 802; 747, first class A2 (window)
9:25 am	Arrive at New York LaGuardia Airport. Take limousine to Waldorf Hotel, 2021 Second Avenue, New York (212-542-6000); guaranteed hotel reservation; confirmation in trip file
1:00 pm	Meeting with Mr. Rogers C. Harper, Jr., President, ACF Corporation at Ninth Gate, 994 Third Avenue, New York (212-776-1420)
7:00 pm	Dinner-meeting at Stewart's Restaurant, 727 Avenue of the Americas, New York, with Mr. Joyce L. Rohrson, Consultant, American Business Systems (212-325-4692)
Tuesday, January 11 (New York City)	
9:30 am	The National Office Systems Conference, City Conference Center, 1004 Central Parkway, New York (212-554-4200)
9:45 am	Presentation: "The Office Environment -- Networking and Today's Automated Office"
1:00 pm	Luncheon with Mr. Raymond L. Bernard, Vice President and General Manager, Wilson Automation, Inc., at the Oakdale City Club, 9250 Fifth Avenue, New York (212-347-3300)
3:00 pm	Tour of Advanced Business Systems, Inc., 125 Seventh Avenue, New York. Contact Person: Ms. Helen Adams, Office Automation Consultant (212-774-1550)
Wednesday, January 12 (New York City to Seoul)	
9:45 am	Leave Waldorf Hotel by limousine for John F. Kennedy Airport
11:55 am	Leave JFK Airport on Korean Air Flight 804, business class, C4 (aisle seat)
Thursday, January 13 (Seoul, Korea)	
3:00 pm	Arrive at Seoul Incheon Int'l Airport. Company limousine will meet you at the baggage claim.

- in connection with~: ~에 관련되어, 관하여
- forthcoming: 다가오는
- attach: 첨부하다
- appointment: 약속
- attachment: 첨부

[수행순서] 반 ___ 학번 _________ 이름 _________ 제출일 _________

다음 수행순서에 알맞게 문서가 작성되었는지 살펴보고 확인 칸에 체크표시하세요.

번호	수행순서	확인
1	문서의 종류를 정한다.	☐
2	서식파일을 연다.	☐
3	문서를 작성한다.	☐
4	초안을 검토한다.	☐
5	상사에게 보고한다.	☐
6	발신인과 발신 정보를 확인하여 발송한다.	☐

보고 Tip:

사장님,
___________씨에게 발송할 _____의 초안을 작성하였습니다.
내용은 ________________________________
_______________________ 건입니다.
검토하시고 수정할 사항이 있으시면 말씀하여 주십시오.

[작성 결과물 체크리스트]

	내용	Yes	No
1	문서 양식에 따른 구성요소가 모두 포함되었는가?	☐	☐
2	본문의 문단 나누기가 적절한가?	☐	☐
3	문서의 전체적 레이아웃이 적절한가? (여백)	☐	☐
4	문서의 모양이 적절한가? (글씨체, 글씨크기, 줄간격 등)	☐	☐
5	오탈자를 확인하였는가?	☐	☐

PART

03

영문서 작성하기

학습목표

- 사용목적에 따른 영문서의 종류에 따라 필요한 구성요소와 형식을 파악할 수 있다.
- 상사의 지시에 따라 정해진 시간 내에 문법과 형식에 맞추어 영문서를 작성할 수 있다.
- 정확한 영문서 작성을 위해 초안을 검토하고 상사의 지시에 따라 수정·보완할 수 있다.

1 자주 사용하는 어휘 · 표현 · 약어 · 제목

(1) 본문에 자주 사용되는 어휘

다음의 단어들은 자주 비즈니스 문서 본문에서 사용된다. 암기해놓으면 유용하다. 일반영어에서와는 다른 의미로 쓰이는 경우도 있으므로 유의하자.

동사

book	예약하다, 장부에 기입하다
confirm	확인하다
deliver	배달하다
enclose	동봉하다
reserve	예약하다

명사

amount	금액
interest	이자, 관심, 관심을 끌다
payment	지급, 지급금액, 결제
quantity	수량
specification	설명서, 사양(仕樣), 명세서
statement	명세서, 계산서
stock	재고, 주식

주문관련

order	주문, 주문하다.
quotation	가격표시, 견적
quotation wanted	견적요망
invoice	송장(물품청구서)
missing order #2322	분실주문번호 2322
defective order	결함 주문
defective shipment	결함 선적품
wrong delivery: order #2322	잘못된 배달: 주문번호 2322

기타

sales report	영업보고서
annual report	연차보고서
special offer	특별 제안(제공)
minutes	회의록
agenda of meeting	회의안건
visit to Seoul	서울방문
business trip	출장

(2) 본문에 자주 사용되는 표현

문서를 작성할 때 통상적으로 자주 사용되는 문장이 있는데, 이를 알아두면 유용하게 사용할 수 있다.

시작하는 문구의 예

- I am writing to inform you that we received your order today.
- I am writing to ask about agents for our products in Korea.
- I am writing to apologize for the wrong order we sent.

- Thank you for your quick reply.
- I am grateful for your great support.

- Please note that the next meeting will be held on Tuesday.
- Please remember that tomorrow, August 15, will be closed for the national holiday in Korea.

- Please see (find) the attached.
- FYI, I am forwarding the below email and attachments.

마무리하는 문구의 예

- I would appreciate if you can reply by tomorrow.
- I look forward to hearing from you.
- Please do not hesitate to contact me if you have any questions.
- Please let me know if you need further information.
- Thank you for your cooperation.
- Sorry for any inconvenience.

본문에 세부사항을 요약하려고 할 때

• Details are as follows.

(3) 이메일 본문에 자주 사용하는 약어

이메일을 사용할 때 약어를 사용하는 것이 가능하다. 약어 사용 시는 상대방이 분명히 약어의 내용을 알 수 있는 경우나 널리 알려진 것으로 사용한다.

ASAP	→	As soon as possible	가능한 빨리
B4	→	Before	~전에
BTW	→	By the way	그런데
c/o	→	care of / carried over	전교 / 이월하다
CUL	→	See you later	나중에 만나자
F2F	→	Face-to-face	대면하여
FITB	→	Fill in the blank	빈칸을 채우시오
FYI	→	For your information	참고로
N/A	→	Not applicable	해당사항 없음
O/S	→	Out of Stock	품절
TNX/Tnx	→	Thanks	감사하다
w/	→	with	~와 함께
w/o	→	without	~없이
W/B	→	will be	~일 것이다
TBA	→	To be announced	추후통지
TBD	→	To be determined	추후결정
PLS	→	Please	해주세요
IMO	→	In my opinion	저의 견해로는
Attn	→	Attention	수신인
A/F	→	As follows	아래와 같다

(4) 본문에 자주 사용하는 제목 목록

제목은 간략하게 작성하고, 본문내용을 유추할 수 있어야 하며, 그러기 위해서는 구체적이어야 한다. 구체적으로 제목을 작성하기 위해서는 숫자(날짜, 제품번호 등)를 이용하면 좋다.

다음의 Subject List를 참고하면 초보자도 도움을 받을 수 있다.

인사

Greetings	인사 드립니다
Happy New Year	새해인사

축하

Congratulations!	축하합니다
Congratulations on your promotion	승진을 축하합니다
Congratulations on Wedding	결혼을 축하합니다

문의, 부탁

Request	정보요청
Question(s) (about~)	~에 관한 문의
Quick Question	간단한 문의

변경, 약속

Schedule change	일정변경
Reservation change	예약변경
Appointment change	약속변경
Appointment cancellation	약속취소
Revision	수정
Update	갱신
Appointment w/ Mr. A	A와의 약속
Dinner w/ Mr. A	A와의 저녁식사

알림, 통지

Announcement	통지
Announcement of Leave of Absence	휴가통지

감사

Thank you for the gift.	선물 감사합니다
Thank you for your reply.	회신에 대한 감사

2 상황별 예문 독해

(1) 알림(ANNOUNCEMENT)

ANNOUNCEMENT 1

Situation 직원들에게 서머타임을 알리고 그에 따른 출퇴근시간을 준수하도록 통보하는 글이다.

To: All Employees
From: "Younghee Kim"<yhkim@korea.co.kr>
Date: Mon, April 30, 20-- 11:07:30
Subject: Summer Office Hours

Dear all,

New summer office hours will be in effect starting Memorial Day and ending Labor Day. We will open one hour earlier (8am) Monday through Friday.

Please note that we consider this summer to be a trial period.

Questions

1. 서머타임 시행기간은 어떻게 되는가?
2. 원래 정규 근무시간은 어떻게 되었었나?

Note

- **summer office hours**: 하계근무시간
- **Memorial day**(Last Monday in May), **Labor day**(1st Monday in September in the US)
- **through**: 쭉~
- **consider**: 고려하다
- **trial period**: 시험기간, 시범기간

ANNOUNCEMENT ②

Situation 서울 사무실에서 직원회의가 있을 예정이며 그에 따른 안건이 있는 경우 담당자 또는 본인에게 보낼 것을 알리는 글이다.

To: Dixon, Robert D.; Woo, Jennifer; Levis, Robert W.; Mok, Wilbur W.; Kramer, Jeffrey; Painter, Corning F.; Delaney, John M.; Allen, William C.; Bones, Graham M.
CC: Matt Cho
From: Eunji Jang
Date: Mon, January 30, 20-- 11:07:30
Subject: Staff meeting – Feb 15

Dear all,

Pls note that the next staff meeting will be held as follows:

- Date: February 15, 20-- (Mon)
- Time: 9:00 a.m.
- Venue: Conference Room I

Agenda will be distributed by Matt Cho next week. If you have any particular issues to discuss, pls submit them to me or Matt Cho.

Rgds,

EJ Jang

Questions

1. 회의 일정은 언제인가?
2. 안건은 누가 배부할 것인가?

Note

- **will be held**: 개최될 것이다
  The meeting will be held.(회의가 열릴 것이다)
- **venue**: 장소
- **agenda**: 안건
- **distribute**: 배부하다, 돌리다
- **submit**: 제출하다
- **Rgds**: Regards의 줄임말

ANNOUNCEMENT 3

Situation 홍콩에 근무하던 Mr. Springford가 싱가포르로 발령이 나서 그 사실을 공지하는 이메일이다.

To: Anthony Bruce <abruce@png.com>
From: J. C. Springford<jcs@johnson.com>
Date: Mon, October17, 20-- 11:07:30
Subject: Singapore relocation

Dear Mr. Bruce,

I would like you to note that I will be relocated to Singapore office at the end of October, effective from November 01. My new address will be:

Johnson & Johnson International
231 Sims Avenue
Singapore 038985
Tel: 65-432-6874(Direct)
Tel: 65-432-6333(Ext. 874)
Tel: 65-432-6018(Secretary: Ms. Jennifer Lee)
Fax: 65-432-6019

Best wishes,

J. C. Springford

Questions

1. Mr. Springford는 언제 싱가포르로 이사하는가?
2. 싱가포르의 새 주소는?
3. 싱가포르 직통 전화번호는 무엇인가?

Note

- **relocation**: 재배치
- **note**: ~에 주목하다, ~에 주의하다
- **I will be relocating to Singapore office at the end of October.**: 10월 말경에 Singapore 사무실로 이전할 예정이다.
- **effective from November 1**: 11월 1일부터 유효한
- **direct**: 여기서는 직통 전화번호를 의미한다.

ANNOUNCEMENT ④

Situation 출장을 가면서 본인에게 보내는 모든 메시지에 자동으로 응답되도록 설정하고 간 메일이다.

To: "All Recipients"
From: "Hanna Kwon"<hanna_kwon@baewha.co.kr>
Date: Wed, July 6, 20-- 18:07:30
Subject: Auto Reply

Dear all,

I will be out of the office and will be back at July 12.
If you need immediate assistance, please contact Ms. SE Choi at sechoi@baewha.co.kr.

Please also note my e-mail address change to (hanna_kwon@baewha.com) as of July 15.

Rgds,

Hanna Kwon

Questions

1. Ms. Kwon은 언제 직무에 복귀하는가?
2. Ms. Kwon을 대신하여 직무를 수행할 사람은 누구인가?
3. Ms. Kwon의 새로운 e-mail주소는 언제부터 유효한가?

Note

- **note**: 주목하다, 주의하다
- **as of July 15**: 7월 15일자부로

(2) 약속(APPOINTMENT)

APPOINTMENT 1

Situation 런던 본사의 Samuel Lewis가 서울지사에서 방문한 Jackie Yang과 함께 할 저녁 약속에 대해 보내는 글이다.

To: "Jackie Yang"<jyang@cellfirst.com>
From: "Samuel Lewis"<slewis@cellfirst.com>
Date: Mon, January 30, 20-- 11:07:30
Subject: Dinner appointment

Dear Jackie,

This is to remind you of our dinner meeting next Thursday, 10th May.

Are you ok at 18:30 at the Plough on Harborne Road? I heard this new restaurant has a terrace and it's fabulous. My treat, of course.

Please confirm and I look forward to seeing you then.

Warm regards,

Sam

Questions

1. 이 글은 무엇을 하고자 하는 글인가?
2. Sam은 Plough레스토랑의 어떠한 점이 좋다고 이야기하고 있는가?
3. 5월 10일 저녁은 누가 대접하고자 하는가?

Note

- **remind A of B**: A에게 B를 상기시키다.
- **terrace**: 테라스
- **restaurant**: 레스토랑
- **fabulous**: 기막히게 좋은
- **My treat**: 내가 대접을 하겠다
- **look forward to + ~ing (혹은 명사형)**: ~을 기대(고대)하다
- **Sam**: Samuel의 약칭

APPOINTMENT ②

Situation 홍콩지사의 Mr. Smith의 비서인 Ann Dunkin이 Steven Roy에게 conference call의 일정에 대해 알려주는 e-mail이다.

To: "Steven Roy"<sroy@cellfirst.com>
From: "Ann Dunkin"<adunkin@cellfirst.com>
Date: Tue, June 27, 20-- 13:07:24
Subject: Conference call

Dear Steven,

This coming Tuesday, 2nd July at 4:00 pm (Hong Kong time), Mr. John Smith will speak on a conference call to you. Please let me know if you are unable to call in or if you will be traveling and calling in from a mobile.

The telephone number, pass code and conference room location will be communicated before the end of the week.

Best regards,

Ann

Questions

1. Mr. Smith는 언제 Steven Roy에게 conference call을 할 예정인가?
2. Mr. Roy가 전화가 불가능할 경우 어떻게 대처해야 하는가?
3. 이번 주말 전에 서로 알아야 할 내용은?

Note

- this coming Tuesday: (보낸 날짜로 보면) 다음주 화요일
- Hong Kong time: 홍콩시각으로
- conference call: 여러 사람이 동시에 전화로 연결되어 이루어지는 회의
- be unable to: ~할 수 없다(=cannot)
- pass code: 식별코드
- before the end of the week: 주말 이전에

▲ Conference call(전화회의)에 사용되는 전화기

APPOINTMENT ③

Situation Office Magazine의 기자 Mr. Rhee가 인터뷰를 위해 Ms. Jang에게 양해를 구하며 약속 날짜와 시간을 물어보는 글이다.

To: "Manok Jang"<ejjang@hanmail.net>
From: "Paulo Rhee"<prhee@officemagazine.com>
Date: Mon, January 30, 20-- 14:47:30
Subject: Appointment for interview

Dear Ms. Jang:

I would like to interview you on the subject at your convenient time. If you could spare about 30 minutes for the next two weeks to meet with me, it would be much appreciated.

Please let me know what date and time would be the most convenient for you, and I will plan to visit you at your office at that time.

I am eagerly looking forward to meeting you in the near future.

Best wishes,

Paulo Rhee

Questions

1. 약속은 어떻게 정하기로 하였는가?
2. 면담 장소는 어디인가?

Note

- on the subject: 그 주제에 대해서
- at your convenient time: 귀하의 편리한 시간에
- spare: 시간을 내다. Do you have spare time?(시간 좀 있으세요?)
  spare time: 여가시간, 여유시간
- for the next two weeks: 앞으로 두 주일 동안에
- eagerly: 간절히
- in the near future: 조만간에, 가까운 시일 내에

APPOINTMENT ④

Situation Office Magazine의 기자 Mr. Rhee가 보낸 이메일에 대한 Ms. Jang의 답글이다.

To: "Paulo Rhee"<prhee@officemagazine.com>
From: "Manok Jang"<ejjang@hanmail.net>
Date: Wed, February 1, 20-- 10:27:14
Subject: [RE] Appointment for interview

Dear Mr. Rhee,

It is very kind of you to ask me an interview for your prestige magazine. I am happy to have a time. Would it be ok to you on February 12 at 11 a.m. for about an hour?

I would appreciate if you could send me a list of your interview questions before we meet.

Best wishes,

M. Jang

Questions

1. Ms. Jang은 언제 인터뷰를 하기를 원하는가?
2. 인터뷰에 할애할 수 있는 시간은 어느 정도 되는가?
3. 인터뷰 전에 Mr. Rhee에게 요청하는 것은 무엇인가?

Note

- It is very kind of you~: 매우 친절하십니다
- prestige: 위신 있는, 명망 있는
- I am happy to~: 기쁘게 하고 싶다
- about an hour: 대략 한 시간

(3) 취소(CANCELLATION)

CANCELLATION 1

Situation 주문한 책 가운데 몇 권의 책자는 구매 취소를 하고 싶다는 글이다.

To: "Customer Service"<wmarcil@yesbook.com>
From: "Hyunjoo Jang"<hjjang@first.com>
Date: Mon, January 30, 20-- 11:07:30
Subject: Cancelling order (Order No. ABC123X)

Dear Customer Service Team,

I ordered five books on January 27, but I'd like to cancel two of them:

1. 'Model Business Letters' by J. T. Williams
2. 'Structures of Social Life' by A. P. Fiske

Please confirm the cancellation by e-mail.

Thanks,

HJ Jang

Questions

1. Ms. Jang이 최초에 주문한 책은 모두 몇 권인가?
2. Ms. Jang이 취소한 책의 제목은 무엇이며 총 몇 권인가?
3. 발신인이 주문 취소 확인을 받기 원하는 방법은?

Note

- **order**: 주문하다, 주문
- **cancel**: 취소하다
- **"Model Business Letters" by J. T. Williams**: J. T. Williams가 쓴 "Model Business Letters"
- **confirm**: ~을 확인하다
- **Please confirm the cancellation.**: 취소 여부를 알려 주세요.
- **by e-mail**: e-mail을 이용하여

CANCELLATION ②

Situation

YESbook의 고객서비스팀(Customer Service Team)에서 앞서 보낸 Ms. Jang의 도서주문 취소 건에 대한 답글이다.

To: "Hyungjoo Jang"<hjjang@first.com>
From: "Customer Service"<wmarcil@yesbook.com>
Date: Tue, January 31, 20-- 10:27:15
Subject: RE: Cancelling order (Order No. ABC123X)

Dear Ms. Jang,

We are sorry to hear that you don't want to purchase those two books. This is to confirm that your order for those two books has been cancelled. The cancellation number is RX23456 for your reference.

Please don't hesitate to contact us if you have any other queries.

Best regards,

YESbook Customer Service Team

Questions

1. 이 e-mail은 왜 작성된 것인가?
2. YESbook 고객센터에 주문취소 관련하여 연락을 하게 된다면, 어떠한 번호를 알려주면 의사소통이 용이해지겠는가?

Note

- purchase: 구매하다
- cancellation number: 주문취소 번호
- for your reference: 참조용으로
- Please don't hesitate to contact us.: 저희에게 편히 연락주세요.
- if you have any other queries: 만약 다른 질문사항이 있으시면

CANCELLATION ③

Situation

Ms. Marott의 비서 Mina가 상사의 서울출장이 취소된 것을 알리며 예약된 호텔을 취소해 달라는 부탁의 글이다.

To: "Jane Ming"<jane_ming@monitor.com>
From: "Mina Kim"<mina_kim@monitor.com>
Date: Wed, August 11, 20-- 16:39:40
Subject: Cancellation

Dear Jane,

I'm sure you are aware that Ms. Marott's trip to Seoul has been cancelled. Would you mind canceling any hotel arrangements you may have made for her?

Many thanks for all your help.

Kind regards,

Mina Kim
Secretary to Hanne Marott

Questions

1. 무엇을 요청하는 e-mail인가?
2. 발신인의 이름과 직책은?

Note

- cancellation: 취소. cancel(취소하다)의 명사형
- be aware of (that): ~을 알고 있다(know)
- mind: 꺼리다, 싫어하다. 동사 ing형을 목적어로 가져온다.
  Would you mind closing the door?(미안하지만 문 좀 닫아 주실래요?)
- hotel arrangement: 호텔예약
- may have pp: (과거의 불확실한 추측을 나타내어) ~했을지도 모른다
- to: (부속, 관련, 관계) ~의 brother to the King 왕의 동생
  She is secretary to the president.(그녀는 사장 비서이다)

CANCELLATION ④

Situation Hanne Marott의 비서 Mina가 보낸 예약 취소와 관련해서 보낸 이메일에 대한 답장이다.

To: "Mina Kim"mina_kim@monitor.com
From: "Jane Ming"jane_ming@monitor.com
Date: Wed, August 11, 20-- 17:28:20
Subject: RE: Cancellation

Dear Mina,

This is to confirm that Ms. Marott's hotel booking has been cancelled. If you need any further help, please let me know it.

Best regards,

Jane

Questions

1. Jane은 Mina에게 왜 위의 이메일을 보내는가?
2. 마지막 문장은 의례적으로 쓰이는 문구이긴 하지만, Jane은 Mina에게 무엇을 알려달라고 이야기하고 있는가?

Note

- This is to confirm that~: 이 글은 ~을 확인하고자 하는 것입니다.
- please let me know~ : ~을 저에게 알려주세요.

(4) 불만(COMPLAINTS)

COMPLAINTS 1

Situation 주문한 제품을 받아보지 못했음에도 불구하고 카드결제가 된 것에 대해 불만을 토로하고 있다.

To: "Customer Service Center"<cscenter@celltech.com>
From: "Eunshil Na"<ena@yahoo.co.kr>
Date: Mon, September 27, 20-- 17:07:39
Subject: Overdue Delivery (Customer No: 1445-908)

Dear Customer Service Center:

On September 6, I ordered an application (Model No. 281 ML-1), and it was supposed to be delivered within 10 days.

It's September 27 and I haven't received it yet. My credit card records show that you charged my account on September 16. If the product has not yet been sent, please deliver it ASAP. If there's any problem, please send an e-mail and explain the reason for the delay.

Eunshil Na

Questions

1. Eunshil Na가 주문한 제품은?
2. 무슨 문제가 발생하였는가?
3. 제품이 아직 발송되지 않은 경우 발신인이 요청한 내용은?

Note

- **overdue**: 늦은, 연착한
- **charge**: (대가, 요금)을 청구하다
- **reason**: 이유, 까닭
- **delay**: 지연, 지체, 연기

COMPLAINTS ②

Situation 수령받은 제품이 제대로 작동되지 않음을 간략히 설명하며 교환·환불을 요구하는 글이다.

To: "Customer Service"<customer@mands.com>
From: "Julie Roberts"<jroberts@hotmail.com>
Date: Thurs, February 20, 20-- 10:11:30
Subject: Defective Product (Order Number: 026-6438)

Dear Customer Service,

On February 18, I ordered a printer (# 342, model 3, white) but I find the printer I received does not match the product testimonial claims.

I'd like to return this printer and refund of my purchase. Please advise me what I have to do for this.

Regards,

J. Roberts

Questions

1. 발신인이 주문했던 제품은?
2. 제품에 어떤 이상이 발생했는가?
3. 발신인이 새로 요청한 내용은?

Note

- **defective**: 결함이 있는, 불완전한
- **match**: 일치하다, 조화를 이루다
- **product testimonial**: 제품설명서
- **claim**: 주장하다
- **refund**: 환불하다

COMPLAINTS 3

Situation

고객으로부터 판매된 제품 문제로 환불을 요청받은 메일을 받고, 사과의 말과 함께 그 환불 절차에 대해 공지하는 글이다.

To: "Julie Roberts"<jrobers@hotmail.com>
From: "Customer Service"<customer@mands.com>
Date: Fri, February 21, 20--09:11:30
Subject: Refund on order 026-6438

Dear Mrs. Roberts,

We are very sorry for giving you inconvenience. We've processed your refund in the amount of USD65.00 for your Order 026-6438.

This refund is for the following item(s):

Item: Printer # 342 (Model 3), Color: white
Quantity: 1

Your refund is being credited as follows:

Visa Credit Card [ending with 6789]: USD65.00

These amounts will be returned to you within 10 business days. Thank you for shopping at MANDs.

Sincerely,

MANDs Customer Service

Questions

1. 고객이 요청한 프린터의 환급금은 얼마인가?
2. 환급금은 어디로 지급이 되는가?
3. 환급금은 대략 언제 지급된다고 하는가?

Note

- We are very sorry for~: 매우 유감스럽게 생각합니다
- inconvenience: 불편
- refund: 환불
- quantity: 수량
- credit: 입금하다, 대변 debit: 인출하다, 차변

(5) 조의(CONDOLENCES)

CONDOLENCES 1

Situation 골절로 입원해 있는 Mr. H. Kim에게 쾌유를 빈다는 Susie Lee의 글이다.

To: "Hyungmin Kim"<hmkim@g-market.com>
From: "Susie Lee"<slee@pos.com>
Date: Mon, January 30, 20-- 11:07:30
Subject: Get Well Soon!

Dear Mr. Kim,

Your assistant, Ms. Choi, told me that you're in the hospital recovering from a fractured leg. She says you'll be back in the office in 10 days and that you're still conducting business in your hospital room via e-mail.

The good news is that our business can wait till you come back. So please use this time to rest and concentrate on getting well.

Wish you speedy recovery,

Susie Lee

Questions

1. 이 e-mail의 취지는?
2. Mr. Kim이 입원하게 된 이유는?
3. 좋은 소식이란 무엇인가?

Note

- **condolences**: 조의
- **get well**: 회복하다
- **assistant**: 보조자, 보좌인
- **recover**: 회복하다, 완쾌하다(**recover from an illness**: 병이 낫다)
- **fractured leg**: 골절된 다리
- **in**: (시간의 경과를 나타낼 때): ~지나면, ~내로
  He will be back in a few days.(그는 수일 내로 복귀할 것입니다)
- **conduct**: (특정한 활동을) 하다
- **via**: (어떤 장소를) 거쳐

CONDOLENCES ②

Situation 직원의 사망소식에 애도를 표하며, 그의 유가족에게 위로의 글을 보내는 글이다.

Dear Mrs. Leap,

I was saddened to learn that Christopher D. Leap has passed away. He was a good friend to me at work, and he will be missed by his colleagues here.

I had the good fortune to work with Chris at EDC Corp. for the last seven years. He was a good mentor to me, willing to take the time to answer my questions and teach me more about our industry. He was always cheerful and pleasant, and his leadership was a great asset to our company.

Pls accept my sincere condolences. May the sorrow of his passing soon be replaced by the peace and comfort of his memory.

With deepest sympathy,

Jinsu Choi
President
EDC Corporation

Questions

1. Mr. Choi는 Christopher와 몇 년간 함께 일한 동료인가?
2. 회사에서 JS Choi의 멘토는 누구였는가?
3. Mr. CD Leap은 어떠한 사람이였는가?

Note

- passed away(=died, be carried away): 사망하다
  사고로 사망 시는 killed in an accident
- colleagues: 동료
- Corp.: Corporation 기업, 법인, 회사
- asset: 자산
- accept one's condolences: 조의를 받다
  cf) extend one's condolences: 조의를 보내다
- may something be replaced by~ : ~로 대체되기를 바란다

CONDOLENCES ③

Situation 갑작스런 건강악화로 약속이 취소되었다는 것을 알고 상대방에게 쾌유를 바란다는 글이다.

To: "Minju Jung"<mjjung@kepco.com>
From: "Andrew Meng"<andrew_meng@citi.com>
Date: Thurs, September 17, 20-- 10:57:30
Subject: Sympathy

Dear Mr. Jung,

When your secretary called this morning to tell me that you would not be able to keep our appointment due to a sudden illness, I was deeply concerned.

Please accept my best wishes for a complete and speedy recovery and hope to see you in the best of your health soon.

Warm regards,

Andrew Meng

Questions

1. A. Meng은 MJ Jung의 소식을 어떻게 접하였는가?
2. Mr. Jung이 약속을 지키지 못한 이유는?

Note

- **sympathy**: 동정, 연민, 조문(弔問), 위문 **a letter of sympathy**: 조문장
- **keep (break) one's appointment**: 약속을 지키다(어기다)
- **concerned**: 걱정하는, 염려하는 **be concerned**: ~을 걱정하다
- **recovery**: (건강의) 회복, 완쾌

(6) 축하(CONGRATULATIONS)

CONGRATULATIONS 1

Situation Brown 씨가 아래직원 Steve의 노고와 성공을 치하하는 글이다.

To: "Steve Chang"<steve_chang@etech.com>
From: "Mathew Brown"<meg_brown@etech.com>
Date: Mon, March 20, 20-- 14:23:34
Subject: Congratulations on your performance!

Dear Steve,

I just received the final sales numbers for the last fiscal year. Your sales increased more than 21%! This is outstanding and I believe you are pleased with the results.

My sincere thanks to your sales team for a great year. Congratulations!

Best wishes,

Mathew Brown

Questions

1. Brown 씨는 Steve에게 무엇을 축하하고 있는가?
2. 위의 글로 미루어보아 Steve가 속한 부서는?

Note

- fiscal year: 회계연도
- increase: 증가하다
- outstanding: 뛰어난

CONGRATULATIONS ②

Situation 새로운 직책에 임명된 동료에게 축하의 글을 보내는 e-mail이다.

To: "Nick Bacon"<n_bacon@e-golf.com>
From: "Kay Kim"<kay_kim@e-golf.com>
Date: Mon, May 30, 20-- 11:07:30
Subject: Congratulations!

Dear Nick,

I have just learned that you have been appointed as a Regional Manager for the Asia/Pacific. Looking back the past years, I know your enthusiasm and experience are the valuable qualities that are needed for this position. I wish every success in managing the branch.

My colleagues join me in sending you our warmest congratulations!

Very best wishes,

Kay Kim
Seoul Branch

Questions

1. 무엇을 축하하는 내용인가?
2. Mr. Bacon의 새로운 직책은?
3. 이 새로운 직책에 꼭 필요한 자질은?

Note

- **learn**: ~을 알다
- **appoint**: 임명하다, 지명하다. **He was appointed as a new manager.**
- **regional manager for the Asia Pacific**: 아시아태평양지역 소장
- **enthusiasm**: 열정, 정열
- **valuable**: 귀중한, 중요한
- **quality**: 자질, 특성
- **wish**: ~을 빌다. **I wish you happiness.**(행복하시길 빕니다)
- **colleague**: 동료, 동업자(=companion)

CONGRATULATIONS ③

Situation 거래처 직원의 승진을 축하하는 글이다.

To: "Meggie Wong"<meggie@dreamtech.com>
From: "MiyoungSohn"<msohn@e-mart.com>
Date: Mon, January 30, 20-- 11:07:30
Subject: Congratulations on your promotion!

Dear Ms. Wong,

I'm very delighted to hear your promotion to a managing director at ABC, Ltd. Congratulations!

I am sure that your expertise and dedication will elevate our business relationship to an even more fruitful level.

We send you our very best wishes for the future.

Best wishes,

M. Sohn

Questions 1. e-mail을 발송하는 목적은?

Note

- **promotion**: 승진
- **expertise**: 전문적인 기술
- **dedication**: 헌신, 봉사
- **elevate**: 높이다, 올리다
- **even (still)**: 비교급을 강조하여 '더욱'의 뜻이 됨.
- **fruitful**: 열매를 많이 맺는, 성과가 높은
- **level**: 수준, 정도

CONGRATULATIONS 4

Situation 승진을 축하하는 편지이다.

186 Part Lane
Brooklyn, NY
USA

BROOKS
DRINKS MACHINES, LTD

February 8, 20--

Mr. Gary Greenspan
Investment Relations Dept.
ACE Capitals
Beulingstratt 23
Amsterdam
The Netherlands

Dear Mr. Greenspan,

I am writing to congratulate you on your appointment as Executive Vice President of ACE Capitals.

I know that you will do a wonderful work in your new position, and I look forward to doing further business with you in the future.

Sincerely yours,

Michael Franks

Questions

1. 수신인 Mr. Greenspan은 어느 나라에 있는 회사에 재직 중인가?
2. 발신인 Mr. Franks는 어느 나라에 있는 회사에 재직 중인가?
3. 수신인이 새로 임명된 직책은?

Note

- congratulate: 축하하다
- appointment: 임명
- Executive Vice President: 부사장, 전무, 상무
- capital: 자본, 자산

(7) 문의(INQUIRES)

INQUIRES 1

Situation 복사기 안내책자를 받아보고 싶다고 부탁하는 글이다.

To: “Chulsoo Kim”<inchung@officeland.com>
From: “Jinsuk Song”<jsong@samjung.co.kr>
Date: Sat, March 30, 20-- 15:37:30
Subject: Inquiry about your brochure

Dear Mr. Kim,

I have a great interest in N-456 photocopier advertised on the front page of “Office for the Future”.

Could you please send me a brochure of that?

A prompt reply would be appreciated.

Regards,

Jinsuk Song
Plant Manager

Questions

1. 편지를 쓴 사람의 직함은?
2. 어떠한 내용을 부탁했는가?
3. 편지 쓴 사람은 요구한 책자의 모델을 어디에서 알게 되었는가?

Note

- **brochure**: 안내책자(pamphlet과 유사)
- **photocopier**: 복사기, copier 또는 copy machine이라고도 함.
- **prompt reply**: 신속한 대답
- **plant manager**: 공장장, 공장책임자

INQUIRES 2

Situation 제품에 대한 견적의뢰서를 요청하는 글이다.

To: "Sean Lee"<sean_lee@bizbaz.com>
From: "Vickie Louise"<vlouise@cleany.com>
Date: Mon, October 3, 20-- 11:07:30
Subject: Quote for price estimation

Dear Mr. Lee,

We are interested in the following model:

- Model: MC-100
- Quantity: 3,200 pieces
- Terms: CIF New York

Can you please quote a price? If a volume discount is available, please indicate that. I would appreciate if you also let us know the delivery time and payment terms.

I look forward to hearing from you soon.

Best regards,

Vickie Louise

Questions

1. 어떤 내용을 문의하는 편지인가?
2. 가격조건은 어떠한 것을 제시했는가?
3. 편지 쓴 사람이 추가로 더 알고 싶어한 내용은?

Note

- **guote a price**: 가격을 제시하라
- **terms**: 조건 **payment terms**: 지불조건
- **CIF**: Cost, Insurance and Freight(운임: 보험료포함 가격)
- **If a volume discount is available**: 수량할인(대량구매할인)이 있다면
(↳ 많이 쓰이므로 문장으로 암기)

INQUIRES ③

Situation 앞의 제품에 대한 견적 의뢰건으로 보낸 이메일에 대한 답장이다.

To: "Vickie Louise"<vlouise@cleany.com>
From: "Sean Lee"<sean_lee@bizbaz.com>
Date: Mon, October 3, 20-- 14:23:30
Subject: Quote Wanted

Dear Ms. Louise,

We are grateful for your inquiry. Followings are the info. you asked:

[Discount Rate]
- Less than 2,000: 5%
- Less than 4,000: 10%
- Less than 7,000: 15%

[Delivery Policy]
- Air mail: Within 5 working days
- Sea mail: Within a month

The cost will be advised later when you give us your exact order quantity and your delivery choice.

Best regards,
Sean

Questions
1. 3,000개 주문 시 할인율은 얼마인가?
2. 배로 주문하면 도착일은 언제인가?

Note
- grateful: 감사하는
- inquiry: 질문, 문의, 조회
- discount rate: 할인율
- less than~: ~보다 적은
- delivery policy: 배송정책
- air mail: 항공편
- sea mail: 선편
- order quantity: 주문수량

INQUIRES ④

Situation 안내책자를 보내줄 수 있는지 문의하는 편지이다.

November 23, 20--

Music Supplies, Ltd.
234 Hinton Road
Birmingham BR6 7PH

Dear Sir or Madam,

Re: Instrument supplies

I am writing about your advertisement in 'Music Monthly'.

Could you please send me your catalogue 'Strings and Instrument Accessories'. I would also like you to contact me to arrange a visit by a sales representative.

I look forward to hearing from you.

Yours faithfully,

H. R. Brown

H. R. Brown, Manager
The Music Shop

Questions

1. Music Supplies 회사를 어디에서 알고 연락을 하고 있는가?
2. 받고 싶은 안내책자의 제목은 무엇인가?
3. 안내책자를 받은 후 Mr. Brown이 원하는 것은 무엇인가?

Note

- **instrument**: 기구, 악기
- **advertisement**: 광고
- **monthly**: 월간의
- **catalogue**: 안내책자
- **strings**: 현악기
- **arrange**: 마련하다, 처리하다, 정리하다
- **sales representative**: 영업담당자

(8) 주문(ORDERS)

ORDERS 1

Situation 잡지 구독신청을 하면서 구독료를 묻고 있는 간단한 e-mail이다.

To: "Rachel Bae"<Rachel_bae@bizworld.com>
From: "Jay Jeon"<jay_jeon@csfb.com>
Date: Mon, January 30, 20-- 11:07:30
Subject: Subscription

Dear Ms. Bae,

I'd like to have a one-year subscription to "Office Pro". I would appreciate if you let me know what to do for subscription.

Best wishes,

Jay Jeon

Questions

1. 발신인이 구독하기를 원하는 잡지 이름은?
2. One-year subscription을 해석해보시오.

Note

- subscription: 구독, 신청, 예약, 응모. 보통은 잡지 따위의 정기 간행물을 예약, 구독함을 뜻하며 정기간행물 명칭 앞에 전치사 to를 붙인다.

ORDERS ②

Situation 모니터를 주문하면서 정확한 구매비용이 어떠한지 묻는 글이다.

To: "Jihye Cha"<jhcha@copierland.com>
From: "Shinae Lim"<salim@hsbc.com>
Date: Wed, March 20, 20-- 09:57:30
Subject: Order (Ref No. 233-23)

Dear Ms. Cha,

We would like to place an order with you for the following quantities and models:

Order	Unit	Price	Total
Monitor No. 32	5	US$500.00	US$2,500.00
Monitor No. 50	5	US$300.00	US$1,500.00

We understand that these charges do not include taxes, customs, shipping and storage charges. We would be grateful if you confirm this order and send an itemization of the additional costs.

Regards,

Shinae Lim

Questions

1. 어떠한 것을 주문하였는가?
2. 수신자에게 요청한 내용은 무엇인가?

Note

- place an order: = order(주문하다)
- quantity: 수량
- monitor: 모니터
- charge: 비용
- customs: 관세
- shipping or storage charges: 선적비 또는 보관비
- grateful: 고마워하는, 감사하는
- itemization of the additional costs: 추가비용의 항목

ORDERS 3

Situation 앞 글에 대한 답신 글로서, 주문 확인과 그에 대한 비용을 알려주는 글이다.

To: “Shinae Lim”<salim@hsbc.com>
From: “Jihye Cha”<jhcha@copierland.com>
Date: Wed, March 20, 20--11:23:14
Subject: Order confirmation (No. 233-23)
Attachment: Order 23323.pdf

Dear Ms. Lim:

This is to confirm your order No. 233-23(our reference number is 2323). Please find the attached for details on shipping and insurance.

Order	Unit	Price	Total
Monitor No. 32	5	US$500.00	US$2,500.00
Monitor No. 50	5	US$300.00	US$1,500.00
			US$4,000.00

Shipping: US$200.00
Insurance: US$100.00

ETD: March 22
ETA: April 1

Regards,
Jihye Cha

Questions

1. 첨부파일에는 어떤 내용이 있는가?
2. 모니터 10대의 총 구매비용은 어떻게 되는가?
3. Ms. Lim은 대략 언제 제품을 받아볼 수 있는가?

Note

- order confirmation: 주문확인(서)
- reference number: 참조번호
- attached file: 첨부된 파일
- details on shipping and insurance: 선적비 및 보험료의 명세
- shipping: 선적비
- insurance: 보험료
- ETD: Estimated Time of Departure(출발예정시간)
- ETA: Estimated Time of Arrival(도착예정시간)

ORDERS ④

Situation 주문한 제품이 단종되었다는 사실을 알리는 편지이다.

CornfieldsPesticides Co. Ltd
59 THE HILL, BURTON SUSSEX BN54 9TJ Tel 01273 52663

November 22, 20--

Ms. Richard Scott
Welsh Garden Suppliers
Cardiff
CF34 2FT

Dear Ms. Scott,

Thank you for your telephone order of November 16.

I'm writing to provide the answers for your inquiries regarding our 'FLY KILLER' spray.

Unfortunately, we have stopped producing this fly spray due to the fact that sales were rather disappointing. However, we are able to supply you with a maximum of 20 boxes from our stocks. If you would like to order these, please could you inform us as soon as possible?

I look forward to your reply.

Yours sincerely,

S. Wollen

Sarah Wollen
Sales Representative

Questions

1. 고객이 주문한 제품은 무엇인가?
2. 제품이 단종된 이유는 무엇인가?
3. Ms. Wollen은 주문한 고객에게 어떠한 제안을 하고 있는가?

Note

- **provide**: 제공하다
- **regarding**: ~에 관하여
- **unfortunately**: 불행히도
- **produce**: 생산하다
- **due to~**: ~때문에
- **rather**: 꽤, 약간, 상당히
- **disappoint**: 실망시키다
- **supply**: 공급하다
- **maximum**: 최고의
- **stock**: 재고
- **inform**: 알리다

(9) 요청(REQUIREMENTS)

REQUIREMENTS 1

Situation 첨부한 파일을 열 수 없어 다시 보내줄 것을 요청하는 글이다.

To: "Jihye Cha"<jhcha@copierland.com>
From: "Shinae Lim"<salim@hsbc.com>
Date: Wed, March 20, 20--11:40:17
Subject: Attachment error

Dear Jihye,

Thanks for e-mailing me the quotation. I can't read the attached file. Could you paste the document onto e-mail and re-send it, please?

Thanks,

Shinae Lim

Questions

1. 무엇을 요청하는 내용인가?
2. 수신인은?
3. e-mail을 보낸 날짜는?

Note

- attachment: 첨부물
- quotation: 견적서
  Thanks for e-mailing me the quotation.
  (견적서를 e-mail로 보내주셔서 감사합니다)
- attached file: e-mail에 첨부된 파일
- paste: 붙이다

REQUIREMENTS ②

Situation 시계를 배송하기 전 그 비용을 먼저 입금시켜 줄 것을 요청하는 글이다.

To: "Junghee Han"<jhhan@gmail.com>
From: "Dongyung Lee"<dylee@csvm.com>
Date: Thu, May 10, 20--09:27:30
Subject: Re: Request a clock

Dear Ms. Han:

Thank you for your e-mail.

Please send us a check or T/T for U$100 and then we can dispatch you the clock(Item No. #3206).

Thank you again for your interest in Specialty Vintage Clocks.

DY Lee
Catalogue Sales Representative
Specialty Vintage Motors

Questions

1. 시계를 받으려면 무엇을 보내야 하는가?
2. 시계의 가격은?

Note

- check: 수표
- T/T: 전신환송금(Telegraphic Transfer)
- dispatch: 급송하다, 급파하다
- interest: 관심
  Thank you for your interest.(귀하의 관심에 감사 드립니다)
- sales representative: 영업대표

REQUIREMENTS 3

Situation

ISTM 잡지 내 광고된 프로그램의 정보를 얻고자 보내는 글이다.

To: "Naomi Wilson"<naomi_wilson@istm.org>
From: "GilsangByun"<gsbyun@lycos.com>
Date: Mon, May 17, 20--15:34:40
Subject: Request for information

Dear Ms. Wilson,

Please send me information about the International Sales Training Program in the May issue of *International Sales Training Magazine*.

I look forward to your reply.

Regards,

Byun, General Manager

Questions

1. Mr. Byun은 몇 월호 잡지를 보고 자료를 요구하는가?
2. 편지 쓴 사람의 직함은?

Note

- May issue: 잡지 등의 '5월호'
- International Sales Training Program: 국제판매 훈련프로그램
- general manager: 부장, 지사장, 총지배인(호텔의 경우)

REQUIREMENTS ④

Situation

매월 카탈로그를 받기 위해 주소록에 본인의 이름을 넣어달라고 요청하는 글이다.

To: "Christine Edwards"<wsong@bizmachine.co.kr>
From: "Younghee Kim"<yhkim@gi.ac.kr>
Date: Mon, January 30, 20-- 11:07:30
Subject: REQ: Catalog

Dear Ms. Edwards:

Please place my name on your mailing list to receive your monthly catalogs regarding business machinery, and let me know if there's any handling charge.

Thank you.

Name: Younghee Kim
Address: Kyongin Academy
45-6 Seorin-dong, Jongro-gu
Seoul 110-714, Korea
CPO Box 1340
Tel 822 397 5000

Questions

1. 수신인은 누구인가?
2. 발신인이 요청한 내용은?
3. 'Let me know if there is any handling charge.'를 해석해보시오.

Note

- **REQ**: Request 요청, 요구
- **mailing list**: 우편 수취자 명단
- **monthly**: 한 달에 한 번 발행되는
- **catalog(catalogue)**: 목록, 카탈로그
- **regarding**: ~에 관해서
- **business machinery**: 사무 기계류
- **charge**: 요금, 대가
- **CPO**: Central Post Office 중앙사서함

(10) 예약(RESERVATION)

RESERVATION 1

Situation

Business.Com의 싱가포르 지사 Mr. Blass는 동료와 함께 서울로 출장 예정이다. 이에 서울지사의 Katie에게 호텔예약을 부탁하는 e-mail이다.

To: "Katie Jung"<kjung@biz.com>
cc: "James Gorman"<jgorman@biz.com>
From: "Mark Blass"<mblass@biz.com>
Date: Tue, June 27, 20--09:17:474
Subject: Hotel Reservation

Dear Katie,

Could you please make reservations for James Gorman and me at the Grand Intercontinental Hotel near the KEPCO office? We would like to have two single rooms on the executive floor.

We expect to arrive in Seoul on 12 July and depart on 15 July (3 nights).

Thanks in advance,

Mark Blass

Questions

1. Mark Blass와 동행하는 사람은 누구인가?
2. Mark가 인터콘티넨탈 호텔에 방을 예약하기 원하는 이유는?
3. 어떤 방을 예약하길 원하는가?
4. 이들의 check-in/check-out 날짜는 어떻게 되는가?

Note

- **make a reservation**: (=reserve) 예약하다
- **single room**: 1인용 침실
- **expect**: 기대하다. 예정이다
  He is expecting you.(그가 당신을 기다리고 계십니다)

RESERVATION ②

Situation Business.Com의 서울지사의 Katie가 싱가포르 지사 Mr. Blass에게 호텔예약이 완료되었음을 알려주는 e-mail이다.

To: “Mark Blass”<mblass@biz.com>
cc: “James Gorman”<jgorman@biz.com>
From: “Katie Jung”<kjung@biz.com>
Date: Tue, June27, 20-- 13:23:24
Subject: Re: Hotel Reservation

Dear Mark:

Hotel reservation you requested is confirmed. Here is your hotel confirmation at the Grand Intercontinental Hotel:

Check in/out: July 12 – July 15
Room Type: Single room on the executive floor.
Number of Rooms: 2 (Two)
Confirmation number: 234343 (James Gorman)
234344 (Mark Blass)

I need to inform your flight schedule to the hotel. Please inform me when it is fixed.

Regards,

Katie Jung

Questions

1. Ms. Jung은 Mark에게 무엇을 요구하고 있는가?
2. 본문에 234343/234344의 번호가 의미하는 것은?

Note

- confirmation: 확인, 확신
- check-in: 입실 check-out: 퇴실
- fix: 고정하다, 결정하다
- when it is fixed: 그것이 확정되면

RESERVATION 3

Situation

Business.Com 싱가포르 지점장인 James Gorden의 비서인 Jamie Wong이 확정된 비행스케줄을 서울지사에 알려주는 e-mail이다.

To: "Katie Jung"<kjung@biz.com>
From: "Jamie Wong"<jwong@biz.com>
Date: Tue, June27, 20-- 13:23:24
Subject: Re[2]: Hotel Reservation

Dear Katie,

Pls arrange a car transfer with the following flights details for Mark and James.

	Date	Flight	ETD / ETA
Singapore-ICN	JUL 11	KE 642	22:35 / 06:05+1
ICN-Singapore	JUL 15	KE 641	12:25 / 17:45

Thanks in advance,

Jamie Wong

Questions

1. 무엇을 요청하는 e-mail인가?
2. Mark와 James는 서울에 언제 도착하는가?
3. 위의 e-mail을 받은 Katie가 해야 할 일은?

Note

- arrange: 준비하다, 조정하다, 정하다
- car transfer: 자동차로 이동, 여기서는 호텔과 공항 간의 자동차로 이동할 수 있도록 자동차를 예약해 달라는 뜻임.
- KE 641/642: 대한항공(Korean Air) 641/642편
- in advance: 미리

RESERVATION ④

Situation 예약 확인을 요청하는 편지이다.

Sun Express

20 GLOUCESTER PLACE
CROYDON CR1 2DH
Tel: 020 8241 9273
Fax 020 8243 1945

July 3, 20--

Ms. Charlotte McEvoy
Western Travel
12 the Crescent
Brinton BR3 5YT

Dear Ms. McEvoy,

Re: Tour 5210

I am writing to confirm that I have booked a holiday for 25 people on the above-mentioned holiday, departing 14 July, in the name of Mr. Daniel Thomas.

Please could you tell your clients that they must check in at Gatwick Airport at 9:30 a.m.

We look forward to doing further business with you.

Yours sincerely,

Evelyn Jones

Evelyn Jones
Bookings Supervisor

Questions

1. 무엇을 요청하는 편지인가?
2. 예약자명은 누구인가?
3. 출발일자는 언제인가?
4. 예약인원은 총 몇 명인가?
5. 위의 e-mail을 받은 Charlotte가 해야 할 일은?

Note

- **book**: 예약하다
- **mention**: 언급하다
- **depart**: 출발하다

(11) 감사(THANK YOU)

THANK YOU ①

Situation 서울에 다녀간 Danaka Smith 씨가 체류하는 동안 도움을 주었던 이미영 씨에게 감사의 글을 보내기 위하여 비서에게 아래의 메모를 주었다.

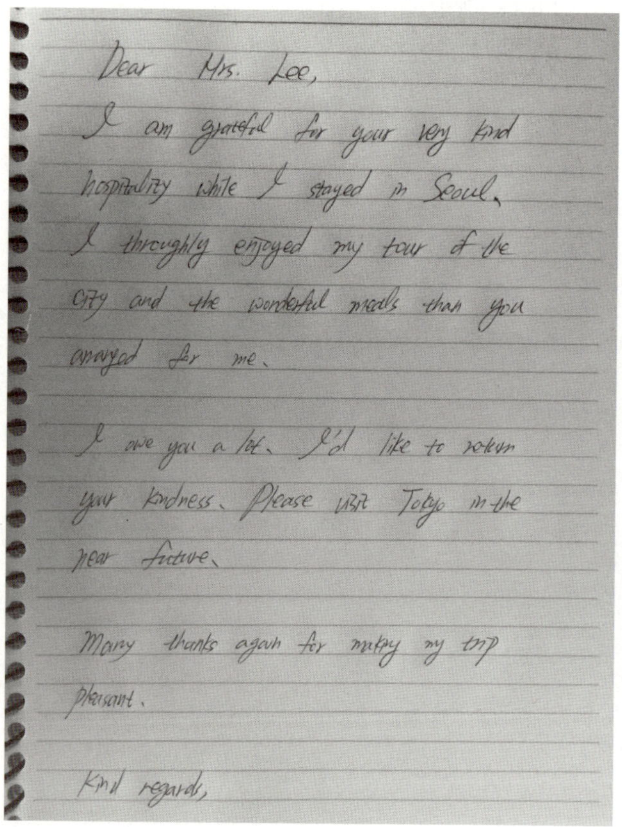

Dear Mrs. Lee,

I am grateful for your very kind hospitality while I stayed in Seoul. I throughly enjoyed my tour of the city and the wonderful meals than you arranged for me.

I owe you a lot. I'd like to return your kindness. Please visit Tokyo in the near future.

Many thanks again for making my trip pleasant.

Kind regards,

Questions

1. 이미영 씨는 Smith 씨에게 무엇을 해주었는가?
2. Smith 씨는 이미영 씨에게 무엇을 해주기 원하는가?

Note

- hospitality: 환대, 친절히 접대함
  Thank you for your hospitality.(친절한 접대에 감사드립니다)
- thoroughly: 전적으로, 완전히
- in the near future: 곧

THANK YOU ②

Situation 스톡홀름에 다녀간 Ms. Lawrence가 체류하는 동안 도움을 주었던 Ms. Klein에게 감사의 뜻으로 보내는 편지이다.

ISLAND WORLD HOLIDAYS
181 North Street
London KY16 2FW
Tel: 020-8768 6090
Fax: 020-8768 9222
www.island.co.uk
sales@island.co.uk

December 2, 20--

Ms. Magarets Klein
Slottsberget 26
Goteborg 41803
Sweden

Dear Ms. Klein,

I would like to thank you for all your help during my stay in Stockholm, and wonderful dinner on the last day of my itinerary. Everything was so delicious.

My trip to Sweden was very impressive, and I look forward to meeting you again on the next annual meeting in London next year. I will be able to show you around the city and return your hospitality.

I have enclosed some photographs during my stay there.

I sincerely appreciate it again.

With regards,

Jennifer Lawrence

Enclosure

Questions

1. Ms. Klein은 Ms. Lawrence에게 무엇을 해주었는가?
2. 이 편지의 동봉물은 무엇인가?
3. Ms. Lawrence는 다음에 어디서 다시 만날 것을 제안하는가?

Note

- **itinerary**: 일정표
- **delicious**: 맛있는
- **impressive**: 인상적인, 인상깊은
- **photograph**: 사진
- **sincerely**: 진심으로

(12) 기타 - 초청장(OTHERS – INVITATION CARD)

Situation

미국 알래스카주와 대한민국의 유대강화를 축하하기 위한 리셉션에 초대한다는 초대장이다.

The Honorable Tony Knowles, Governor, the State of Alaska
&
Mrs. Susan Knowles
request the pleasure of your company
at a reception
to honor the growing ties
between the Republic of Korea and State of Alaska
on Monday,
the 23rd day of September, 20--,
from 6 until 8 P.M.

R.S.V.P. 739-8058/9 (Ms. Susan Kim) — The Grand Ballroom
The favor of a reply is requested by September 13. — Westin Chosun Hotel

Questions

1. Reception의 주최자는 누구인가?
2. Reception을 개최하는 목적은?
3. Reception의 일시와 장소는?

Note

- **The Honorable Tony Knowles, Governor, the State of Alaska**: 알래스카주의 주지사인 Tony Knowles 씨. The Honorable은 미국의 상하원 의원 및 주의원의 성명 앞에 붙이는 경칭임.
- **request**: 청하다, 요청하다
- **reception**: 환영회, 리셉션 (**hold reception** 환영회를 베풀다)
- **honor**: 경의를 표하다, 기리다, 축하하다
- **RSVP(reply if you please)**: 참석 여부를 알려달라는 불어의 약어로 초청장에서 많이 쓰이는 표현이므로 반드시 알아두어야 함.
  * **RSVP** 밑에 기재된 연락처로 참석 여부를 알려주어야 함.
  cf) *regret only*(불참 시에만 연락주세요)
- **grand ballroom**: 대연회장

3 수행실습

수행체계도

문서의 수・발신 정보를 확인한다.

↓

영문서 서식을 정한다.

↓

선택한 서식파일을 연다.

↓

문서의 초안을 작성한다.

↓

상사에게 보고하여 검토받는다.

↓

검토사항을 반영하여 수정・보완한다.

↓

상사의 결재를 받는다.

↓

수・발신 정보에 따라 발송한다.

수행 1

박 부사장*(Jason Park, Vice-President)은 다음 사항을 우리 회사의 모든 직원들(All employees)에게 고지하라는 이메일을 이수연(Sooyeon Lee) 비서에게 보냈다. 적절한 문서서식을 선택하여 문서를 발송하되, 수행순서에 따라 업무를 수행하세요.

> 제목 : New Employee Announcement Date : 오늘 날짜
>
> I am pleased to announce the addition of Ms. Yeona Han to Air Products Korea in the position of Marketing Director effective 1 June. Ms. Han brings with her over 18 years of F&B industry experience, including 6 years in Research/QC/Planning with Korea Chemical and 12 years in global F&B companies, most recently as sales and marketing manager at Rohm and Hass Korea. ¶Ms. Han's extensive knowledge of the F&B industry will be very valuable in expanding our future business. Ms. Han will be primarily responsible for strategic planning, new product development, profitability, pricing and sales training. Ms. Han has a chemical engineering degree from Daehan University, Korea. Reporting to Ms. Han will be Mr. G. Kim and Mr. J.M. Shim. Please join me in welcoming Ms. Han to Global FNB Korea.

문서 작성 Tip

¶ : 교정부호. 새로운 문단으로 나누라는 뜻임

* 제이슨 박은 글로벌 식음료(Food & Beverage) 유통회사인 Global FNB Korea의 부사장(Vice-President)이라는 가상인물이다.

[수행순서] 반 ____ 학번 __________ 이름 __________ 제출일 __________

1. 다음 수행순서에 알맞게 문서가 작성되었는지 살펴보고 확인 칸에 체크표시하세요.

번호	수행순서	확인
1	문서의 수·발신 정보를 확인한다.	☐
2	영문서 서식을 정한다.	☐
3	선택한 서식파일을 연다.	☐
4	문서의 초안을 작성한다(문서의 내용을 확인한다).	☐
5	상사에게 보고하여 검토받는다.	☐
6	수정사항을 반영하여 완성한다. ★ 수정사항:	
		☐
		☐
		☐
		☐
		☐
		☐
		☐
		☐
		☐
		☐
7	상사의 결재를 받는다.	☐
8	수·발신 정보에 따라 발송한다.	☐

2. 본문의 내용을 아래에 해석하세요.

3. 김영희 비서가 작성한 초안을 확인한 박 부회장은 작성자와 입력자 표시를 따로 하라는 지시를 내리며 바로 보내도 좋다고 하였다. 문서를 작성하세요.

수행 2

박 부사장(Jason Park, Vice-President)은 아래 문서의 오류를 수정하여 발송하라는 지시를 하셨다. 발송 시 pdf 파일로 변환 후 이메일에 첨부하여 발송하라고 지시하였다. 수행순서에 따라 업무를 수행하세요.

※참고: 틀린 부분(대문자, 구두점, 문법, 철자)

GLOBAL FNB KOREA

123 Hyorong-ro, Seocho-gu
Seoul 16351, Korea
Tel. (822) 343-2328 Fax. (822) 343-2222

June 23, 20--

Olson's Office Furniture
15 Watergate Plaza
new Orleans, LA 34343

Reference Number: PO 434-212A

Deer sir:

The purchase order referenced above are enclosed

Please process the order as soon as possible If you has any questions, please contact me or Ms. m. Whiting, Head of Logistics at (303) 343-2389

Thank you for your atention.

sincerely

William Rogers

jason park
Vice-President

Enclosure

문서 작성 Tip

- pdf 파일로 저장하기
- MS Word: 다른 이름으로 저장>pdf로 저장하기
- 한글: 파일>pdf로 저장하기

[수행순서] 반 ___ 학번 ________ 이름 ________ 제출일 ________

1. 다음 수행순서에 알맞게 문서가 작성되었는지 살펴보고 확인 칸에 체크표시하세요.

번호	수행순서	확인
1	문서의 수·발신 정보를 확인한다.	☐
2	영문서 서식을 정한다.	☐
3	선택한 서식파일을 연다.	☐
4	문서의 초안을 작성한다(문서의 내용을 확인한다).	☐
5	상사에게 보고하여 검토받는다.	☐
6	수정사항을 반영하여 완성한다. ★ 수정사항:	
		☐
		☐
		☐
		☐
		☐
		☐
		☐
		☐
		☐
		☐
7	상사의 결재를 받는다.	☐
8	수·발신 정보에 따라 발송한다.	☐

2. 본문의 내용을 아래에 해석하세요.

수행 3

박 부사장(Jason Park, Vice-President, Global FNB Corp.)에게 다음과 같은 지시를 받았다. 수행순서에 따라 업무를 수행하세요.

김 비서님,
메모의 내용으로
문서를 발송하세요.
발송할 곳 주소도
첨부합니다.

Thank you for your letter.

We are very surprised that you are not going to deliver the coffee and tea that we ordered until the end of the month. We have now found a new supplier, so please cancel our order with you.

We are sorry to tell you that we do not intend to do any further business with you because of the problems we have had.

Peter Geeson, Manager, Arabica Coffee & Tea,
Broadway 340, New York, NY 10002

문서 작성 Tip

발신인: Jason Park, Vice-President, Global FNB Korea, 123 Hyorong-Ro, Seocho-Gu, Seoul, 16351, Korea

- deliver: 배달하다
- supplier: 공급자
- further: 그 이상의
- the end of month: 월말
- intend: ~할 작정이다, 의도하다

[수행순서]

반 ____ 학번 __________ 이름 __________ 제출일 __________

1. 다음 수행순서에 알맞게 문서가 작성되었는지 살펴보고 확인 칸에 체크표 시하세요.

번호	수행순서	확인
1	문서의 수·발신 정보를 확인한다.	□
2	영문서 서식을 정한다.	□
3	선택한 서식파일을 연다.	□
4	문서의 초안을 작성한다(문서의 내용을 확인한다).	□
5	상사에게 보고하여 검토받는다.	□
6	수정사항을 반영하여 완성한다. ★ 수정사항:	
		□
		□
		□
		□
		□
		□
		□
		□
		□
		□
7	상사의 결재를 받는다.	□
8	수·발신 정보에 따라 발송한다.	□

2. 본문의 내용을 아래에 해석하세요.

수행 4

박 부사장(Jason Park, Vice-President)은 한국을 방문할 Mr. Steve Cowell의 일정표를 보내드리라고 지시하였다. 적절한 문서서식을 선택하여 본문을 작성한 후 Mr. Cowell에게 일정표를 첨부파일(동봉물)로 발송하세요. 수행순서에 따라 업무를 수행하세요.

ITINERARY

Visiting Customer in Korea
Prepared for Mr. Steve Cowell

Day & Time	Schedule	Objectives
Tuesday, November 25		
09:30AM	Leave for Hyundai Factory / Ichon	Improvement plan of SW & HW
10:30AM	To visit Hyundai Research Center *Attendees: D.D.Lee/Process Asst. Sr. Mgr. J.S. Park/Mgr.H.S.Lee/Asst. Mgr. H.C.Kang/Asst. Mgr.	
01:30PM	To visit Hyundai Factory Site 3 *Attendees: K.J. Lee/Asst. Sr. Mgr. B.S. Seo/Mgr. D.H. Jang/Asst. Mgr. C.W.Jang, S.Y.Ji	
03:00PM	To visit Hyundai Factory Site 6 *Attendees: B.D.Kwak/Asst. Sr. Mgr. S.K.Kim/Manager S.H.Kim, S.W.Oh	
Wednesday, November 26		
10:00AM	Leave for Samsung/Kihung Visit Samsung Electronics at (Production Engineering Plan)(PEP)	Discuss the free demo
03:00PM	Visit LGS R&D *Attendees: D.H. Lee Dr. J.S. Lee, Dr. J.H. Ha	Discuss the module evaluation
Thursday, November 27		
09:00AM	Leave for Daewoo/Kuro	Process develop of product
10:00AM	Visit Daewoo R&D *Attendees: J.B. Kim/Mgr. J.M. Kim/Asst. Mgr.	Wrap-up meeting

- **Itinerary**: 여행일정표
- **Leave**: 출발하다
- **Attendees**: 참석자

문서 작성 Tip

- 본문에 첨부파일이 있음을 표시하기

[수행순서] 반 ____ 학번 __________ 이름 __________ 제출일 __________

1. 다음 수행순서에 알맞게 문서가 작성되었는지 살펴보고 확인 칸에 체크표시하세요.

번호	수행순서	확인
1	문서의 수·발신 정보를 확인한다.	☐
2	영문서 서식을 정한다.	☐
3	선택한 서식파일을 연다.	☐
4	문서의 초안을 작성한다(문서의 내용을 확인한다).	☐
5	상사에게 보고하여 검토받는다.	☐
6	수정사항을 반영하여 완성한다. ★ 수정사항:	
		☐
		☐
		☐
		☐
		☐
		☐
		☐
		☐
		☐
		☐
7	상사의 결재를 받는다.	☐
8	수·발신 정보에 따라 발송한다.	☐

2. 날짜별 일정을 간략히 요약해보세요.

수행 5

박 부사장(Jason Park, Vice-President)은 다음의 내용으로 해당자들에게 문서를 발송하라고 지시하였다. 수행순서에 따라 업무를 수행하세요.

메신저 Talk

부사장님

다음 달 16일 개최되는 AHA 미팅 참석자들에게 회의 공지 부탁해요.

나

네, 알겠습니다~.

부사장님

시간: 오전 10시~정오
장소: 사내 A회의실(Conference room A)
안건: 추후공지
RSUP는 다음 달 5일까지

나

네, 부사장님~!

문서 작성 Tip

회의 통지문 작성 시 필수 구성요소

- 일시: date / time
- 장소: venue
- 의제: agenda
- 참석 여부: RSVP

Subject: 제목삽입

Contents:

Dear all,

시작하는 문구

회의를 공지하는 내용(Announcement 참조)

마치는 문구

Best regards,
발신자 이름(비서 이름)

[수행순서] 반 ____ 학번 __________ 이름 __________ 제출일 __________

다음 수행순서에 알맞게 문서가 작성되었는지 살펴보고 확인 칸에 체크표시하세요.

번호	수행순서	확인
1	문서의 수·발신 정보를 확인한다.	□
2	영문서 서식을 정한다.	□
3	선택한 서식파일을 연다.	□
4	문서의 초안을 작성한다(문서의 내용을 확인한다).	□
5	상사에게 보고하여 검토받는다.	□
6	수정사항을 반영하여 완성한다. ★ 수정사항:	
		□
		□
		□
		□
		□
		□
		□
		□
		□
		□
7	상사의 결재를 받는다.	□
8	수·발신 정보에 따라 발송한다.	□

수행 6

아래의 사항을 보고 적절한 형식의 문서로 작성하시오. 수행순서에 따라 업무를 수행하세요.

수신인: F. Basuki, basuki@jfkurnishing.com
발신인: Jennifer Long, jlong@intercitybank.com

제목: Order No. 2789
내용:

Thank you for your letter of April 24.

I am writing about your letter concerning the above order for some office furniture.

Unfortunately, we have not yet received the filing cabinets which were a part of this order. We would be grateful if you could deliver these as soon as possible or refund our money.

We look forward to hearing from you.

[수행순서] 반 ____ 학번 __________ 이름 __________ 제출일 __________

1. 다음 수행순서에 알맞게 문서가 작성되었는지 살펴보고 확인 칸에 체크표 시하세요.

번호	수행순서	확인
1	문서의 수·발신 정보를 확인한다.	☐
2	영문서 서식을 정한다.	☐
3	선택한 서식파일을 연다.	☐
4	문서의 초안을 작성한다(문서의 내용을 확인한다).	☐
5	상사에게 보고하여 검토받는다.	☐
6	수정사항을 반영하여 완성한다. ★ 수정사항:	
		☐
		☐
		☐
		☐
		☐
		☐
		☐
		☐
		☐
		☐
7	상사의 결재를 받는다.	☐
8	수·발신 정보에 따라 발송한다.	☐

2. 본문의 내용을 아래에 해석하세요.

수행 7

상사가 아래의 메모를 보고 구매주문서를 작성하라고 지시하였다. 수행순서에 따라 업무를 수행하세요.

MEMORANDUM

To : Sarah Wollen, Purchasing Dept.
From : Paul W. Meeks, Marketing Manager
Date : August 12, 20--
Subject : Supplies Purchasing
Reference : Cannon Catalog Spring 20--

Please prepare a purchase order ASAP for the following.

Item Specifications:

ITEM	STOCK NO.	QUANTITY
Notebook	N1245	4
Transparency	N3489	5
Printout Paper	P1290	5

UNIT COST(USD)	TOTAL COST(USD)
4.50	18.00
40.00	200.00
10.00	50.00

Subtotal	**268.00**
Shipping & Handling (10%)	**26.80**
TOTAL	**USD 294.80**

Charge the total to the Marketing Dept.

* USD: US Dollar

PURCHASE ORDER

Addison Corporation
47 Federal Street
P.O.Box 281
Springfield, MA 01102
TEL. (413)731-5979

Vendor : Cannon Corporation
234 South Street
New York, NY 10010

Ship To :
(use above address unless otherwise indicated)

Reference : Cannon Spring Catalog

Bill To :
(use above address unless otherwise indicated)

Delivery Date : ASAP

Item Specifications:

ITEM	STOCK NO.	QUANTITY
Notebook	N1245	4
Transparency	N3489	5
Printout Paper	P1290	5

UNIT COST(USD)	TOTAL COST(USD)
4.50	18.00
40.00	200.00
10.00	50.00

Subtotal	**268.00**
Shipping & Handling (10%)	**26.80**
TOTAL	**USD 294.80**

Prepared by: ____________ Approved by: ____________
Date Prepared: ____________ Date Approved: ____________

cc: Jane Stone, Accounting

- Purchase Order: 구매주문서

- Vendor: 매도인
- Reference: 참조
- Ship To: 배송지
- Bill To: 청구지

금액은 가운데 정렬이 아니라 자릿수를 정렬되게 한다.

- Prepared by: 문서작성자
- Date prepared: 문서작성일
- Approved by: 결재자
- Date approved: 결재일

[수행순서] 반 ____ 학번 __________ 이름 __________ 제출일 __________

1. 다음 수행순서에 알맞게 문서가 작성되었는지 살펴보고 확인 칸에 체크표시하세요.

번호	수행순서	확인
1	문서의 수·발신 정보를 확인한다.	☐
2	영문서 서식을 정한다.	☐
3	선택한 서식파일을 연다.	☐
4	문서의 초안을 작성한다(문서의 내용을 확인한다).	☐
5	상사에게 보고하여 검토받는다.	☐
6	수정사항을 반영하여 완성한다. ★ 수정사항:	
		☐
		☐
		☐
		☐
		☐
		☐
		☐
		☐
		☐
		☐
7	상사의 결재를 받는다.	☐
8	수·발신 정보에 따라 발송한다.	☐

2. 구매물품이 무엇인지, 각 구매항목에 따른 주문량과 총 구매비용이 어떻게 되는지 설명해보세요.

수행 8

상사가 휴가 중에 본인의 다음 출장 일정을 알려달라는 연락을 하셨다. 다음의 이티켓 (p.154)을 참조하여 항공예약 일정을 알리는 문서를 작성하세요. 수행순서에 따라 업무를 수행하세요.

Subject: 제목삽입

Attachment: E-ticket

Contents:

Dear Mr. ○○○,

시작하는 문구

항공일정(Reservation을 참조하여 정리)

마치는 문구

Best regards,

발신자 이름(비서 이름)

WikiAirlines

YOUR TICKET-ITINERARY

YOUR BOOKING NUMBER : WXIKXI

Flight	From		To		Aircraft	Class/Status
WK 2200	Montreal-Trudeau (YUL) Thu May-04-2006	17:15	Frankfurt (FRA) Fri May-05-2006	06:30+1	333	Y Confirmed
WK 2495	Frankfurt (FRA) T1 Fri May-05-2006	07:50	Amsterdam (AMS) Fri May-05-2006	09:00	321	Y Confirmed
WK 2293	Munich (MUC) T2 Mon May-22-2006	15:30	Montreal-Trudeau (YUL) Mon May-22-2006	17:50	340	Y Confirmed

Passenger Name	Ticket Number	Frequent Flyer Number	Special Needs
(1) JONES, JOHN/MR.	012-3456-789012	000-123-456	Meal: VGML

Purchase Description	Price	
Fare (LLXSOAR, LLXGSOAR)	CAD	558.00
Canada - Airport Improvement Fee		15.00
Canada - Security Duty		17.00
Canada - GST #1234-5678		1.05
Canada - QST #12345-678-901		1.20
Germany - Airport Security Tax		18.38
Germany - Airport Service Fees		37.76
Fuel Surcharge		161.00
Total Base Fare (per passenger)		809.39
Number of Passengers		1
TOTAL FARE	CAD	809.39

Ticket is non-endorsable, non-refundable
Changes allowed, subject to availability,
no later than 2 hours before departure.
Please read carefully all fare restrictions.

Have a pleasant flight!

Paid by Credit Card XXXX-XXXX-XXXX-1234

[수행순서] 반 ___ 학번 _________ 이름 _________ 제출일 _________

1. 다음 수행순서에 알맞게 문서가 작성되었는지 살펴보고 확인 칸에 체크표시하세요.

번호	수행순서	확인
1	문서의 수·발신 정보를 확인한다.	□
2	영문서 서식을 정한다.	□
3	선택한 서식파일을 연다.	□
4	문서의 초안을 작성한다(문서의 내용을 확인한다).	□
5	상사에게 보고하여 검토받는다.	□
6	수정사항을 반영하여 완성한다. ★ 수정사항:	
		□
		□
		□
		□
		□
		□
		□
		□
		□
		□
7	상사의 결재를 받는다.	□
8	수·발신 정보에 따라 발송한다.	□

2. 제시된 e-ticket(p.154)을 보고 다음 출장지는 어디인지 예측해보고, 그 일정에 대해 설명해보세요.

수행 9

유나이티드 항공의 Peter Ranger 씨가 우리 대사관에서 주최하는 행사의 초청장을 분실하였다고 하면서 다시 보내달라는 요청을 하였다. 초청장은 행사의 출입증이므로 반드시 소지하고 있어야 한다. 다음의 정보를 이용하여 문서를 발송하세요. 수행순서에 따라 업무를 수행하세요.

- 수신인: Peter Ranger, United Airlines, 260, Haneul-gil, Gangseo-gu, Seoul, Korea
  Tel: (+822) 2656-2001 Fax (+822) 2656-2002
- 발신인: John Blake, U.S. Embassy, Seoul, 188, 10, Chung-dong, Chung-ku, Seoul, Korea
  Tel: (+822) 397-4908 Fax (+822) 397-4909

On the occasion of United Airlines' launch of its Seoul-to-San Francisco route

The Ambassador of the United States of America
Alexander Vershbow
and Mrs. Lisa Vershbow
request the pleasure of your company at a

"See America Celebration"

Reception on Wednesday, March 15, 2017
at 6:30 p.m.

RSVP
02-397-4908/4324

Ambassador's Residence
10, Chung-dong, Chung-ku

Please present this invitation and personal identification at the entrance.
This invitation is not transferable.

SEE AMERICA

UNITED
20 Years of Asia Pacific Flying

U.S. COMMERCIAL SERVICE
United States of America
Department of Commerce

[수행순서]

반 ___ 학번 __________ 이름 __________ 제출일 __________

1. 다음 수행순서에 알맞게 문서가 작성되었는지 살펴보고 확인 칸에 체크표 시하세요.

번호	수행순서	확인
1	문서의 수·발신 정보를 확인한다.	□
2	영문서 서식을 정한다.	□
3	선택한 서식파일을 연다.	□
4	문서의 초안을 작성한다(문서의 내용을 확인한다).	□
5	상사에게 보고하여 검토받는다.	□
6	수정사항을 반영하여 완성한다. ★ 수정사항:	
		□
		□
		□
		□
		□
		□
		□
		□
		□
		□
7	상사의 결재를 받는다.	□
8	수·발신 정보에 따라 발송한다.	□

2. 초청장의 내용을 아래에 설명하세요.

수행 10

상사가 다음 이메일에 대한 회신을 보내라고 지시하였다. 답신을 위해 필요한 정보를 검색한 후 회신을 작성하세요. 수행순서에 따라 업무를 수행하세요.

Subject: 제목삽입

Contents:

Please help me to extend or reserve a room. As the project schedule is overdue, I need to stay more in Seoul.

My room at InterContinental is up to this coming Monday, 20th January. I tried to extend my booking but the hotel told me there is no available room.

Please select a hotel near the project place. I need a room to 2nd of February.

Many thanks I will try to call you in the afternoon. Thank you.

- extend: 연장하다
- available: 가능한
- overdue: 늦은

문서 작성 Tip

위의 이메일에 대한 답신으로 임의로 호텔 사이트(예: 신라, 하얏트, 힐튼, 리츠칼튼, 그랜드 인터콘티넨탈 등)에 들어가서 다음의 정보를 검색하고 답장을 작성해보세요(Reservation ② 예문을 참조하세요).

① 호텔 이름
② 예약하고자 하는 날짜(Dates for Check-in, Check-out)
③ 객실 유형(Room type)
④ 객실 요금(Room rate)
⑤ 예약번호(Confirmation number): 임의로 작성함.

[수행순서]

반 ___ 학번 _________ 이름 _________ 제출일 _________

1. 다음 수행순서에 알맞게 문서가 작성되었는지 살펴보고 확인 칸에 체크표시하세요.

번호	수행순서	확인
1	문서의 수·발신 정보를 확인한다.	□
2	영문서 서식을 정한다.	□
3	선택한 서식파일을 연다.	□
4	문서의 초안을 작성한다(문서의 내용을 확인한다).	□
5	상사에게 보고하여 검토받는다.	□
6	수정사항을 반영하여 완성한다. ★ 수정사항:	
		□
		□
		□
		□
		□
		□
		□
		□
		□
		□
7	상사의 결재를 받는다.	□
8	수·발신 정보에 따라 발송한다.	□

2. 본문의 내용을 아래에 해석하세요.

수행 11

박지수(Jisoo Park) 상사는 송미나(Mina Song) 비서에게 여러 장의 문서와 고객 명함을 주며 고객에게 문서를 바로 보내줄 것을 부탁하였다. 단, 문서가 컴퓨터에 남지 않도록 하였으면 좋겠다는 고객의 요청이 있었다는 말씀을 더하였다. 어떤 방법으로 문서를 전달할지 생각하여 필요한 영문서를 작성하세요.

A COMPANY

David Lewis
Managing Director
Asia Pacific Division

A Company
24 Flr. A Main Bldg.
134 Hanrogil, Jongnogu
Seoul, 03037 Republic of Korea
Tel. 82-2- 123-4567
Fax. 82-2- 123-4568
Email. dlewis@acom.co.kr

총 15매 문서

[수행순서] 반 ____ 학번 __________ 이름 __________ 제출일 __________

1. 다음 수행순서에 알맞게 문서가 작성되었는지 살펴보고 확인 칸에 체크표 시하세요.

번호	수행순서	확인
1	문서의 수・발신 정보를 확인한다.	□
2	영문서 서식을 정한다.	□
3	선택한 서식파일을 연다.	□
4	문서의 초안을 작성한다(문서의 내용을 확인한다).	□
5	상사에게 보고하여 검토받는다.	□
6	수정사항을 반영하여 완성한다. ★ 수정사항:	
		□
		□
		□
		□
		□
		□
		□
		□
		□
		□
7	상사의 결재를 받는다.	□
8	수・발신 정보에 따라 발송한다.	□

2. 제시된 상사의 지시업무를 수행하는 데에 주의해야 할 점이 무엇인지 설명 하세요.

수행 12

이미영 비서의 상사, 마크 리(Mark Li) 전무는 '프로젝트 타이거'팀에게 다음 주 목요일 화상회의(Video Conference) 일정에 대해 통보해 줄 것을 지시하며, 그 일정 통보를 상사 본인도 함께 받았으면 좋겠다고 말하였다. 화상회의 일정 등에 관한 사항은 다음과 같다.

Project TIGER
Video Conference

Date: October 20(Thur)

Time: 10:30 AM(Seoul Time)

Tel: 82-2-370-4567

Meeting Room: Conference Room 2

다음은 화상회의 참석예정자 명단입니다.

Mark Li(markli@kokotech.co.kr)	홍길동(gdhong@kokotech.co.kr)
Sam Jones(sjones@kokotech.co.kr)	김이영(eyongk@kokotech.co.kr)

[수행순서]

반 ____ 학번 __________ 이름 __________ 제출일 __________

1. 다음 수행순서에 알맞게 문서가 작성되었는지 살펴보고 확인 칸에 체크표시하세요.

번호	수행순서	확인
1	문서의 수・발신 정보를 확인한다.	☐
2	영문서 서식을 정한다.	☐
3	선택한 서식파일을 연다.	☐
4	문서의 초안을 작성한다(문서의 내용을 확인한다).	☐
5	상사에게 보고하여 검토받는다.	☐
6	수정사항을 반영하여 완성한다. ★ 수정사항:	
		☐
		☐
		☐
		☐
		☐
		☐
		☐
		☐
		☐
		☐
7	상사의 결재를 받는다.	☐
8	수・발신 정보에 따라 발송한다.	☐

2. 본문의 내용을 아래에 해석하세요.

수행 13

김대한(Daehan Kim) 전무는 비서에게 본인이 쓴 초안을 A컴퍼니 데이비드 루이스 전무(p.166 명함 참조)에게 보내는 비즈니스 레터를 작성해 달라고 지시를 하였다. 다음은 비서가 김 전무의 초안을 읽고 작성한 것이다. 상사에게 읽기 어려운 단어를 확인한 후 Modified-block Style 비즈니스 레터를 완성해보세요.

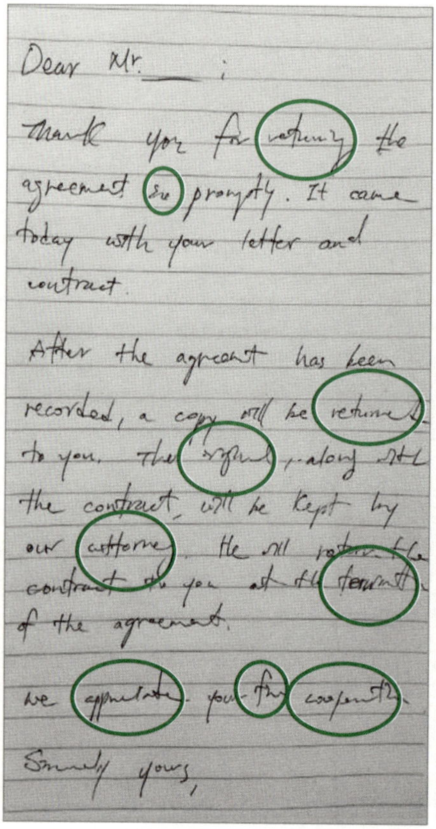

Dear Mr.___ ;

Thank you for returning the agreement so promptly. It came today with your letter and contract.

After the agreement has been recorded, a copy will be returned to you. The original, along with the contract, will be kept by our attorney. He will return the contract to you at the termination of the agreement.

We appreciate your fine cooperation.

Sincerely yours,

Dear Mr.______:

Thank you for returning the agreement so promptly. It came today with your letter and contract.

After the agreement has been recorded, a copy will be re------ to you. The o------- along with the contract, will be kept by our a-------. He will return the contract to you at the termi------ of the agreement.

We app------- your fi--- coo--------.

Sincerely yours,

상사에게 확인받을 곳을 표시한 초안

[수행순서] 반 ____ 학번 __________ 이름 __________ 제출일 __________

1. 다음 수행순서에 알맞게 문서가 작성되었는지 살펴보고 확인 칸에 체크표 시하세요.

번호	수행순서	확인
1	문서의 수·발신 정보를 확인한다.	☐
2	영문서 서식을 정한다.	☐
3	선택한 서식파일을 연다.	☐
4	문서의 초안을 작성한다(문서의 내용을 확인한다).	☐
5	상사에게 보고하여 검토받는다.	☐
6	수정사항을 반영하여 완성한다. ★ 수정사항:	
		☐
		☐
		☐
		☐
		☐
		☐
		☐
		☐
		☐
		☐
7	상사의 결재를 받는다.	☐
8	수·발신 정보에 따라 발송한다.	☐

2. 본문의 내용을 아래에 해석하세요.

수행 14

다음은 받아야 할 선적이 다 오지 않은 것에 대한 불만(complaint)의 내용을 상대 회사에 보내고자 작성한 초안이다. 상사는 초안을 사내 이메일로(비서에게) 보내며 상대 회사 담당자와 관련 문건번호를 찾아 완성하여 보낼 것을 지시하며 그 문건을 본인에게도 함께 보내라고 말씀하셨다. 또한 문서 작성자와 입력자 표시를 할 것을 요청하였다. 급한 용건이므로 조속히 처리되어야 한다고 덧붙이셨다. 적절한 영문서 서식을 선택하여 영문서를 완성하세요(송장번호와 날짜를 임의로 작성해보고, 상사와 비서의 정보는 친구와 교류하여 정하여본다).

비서가 상사에게 받은 초안은 다음과 같다.

Dear ______,

Yesterday we received your shipment of one dozen King printing machines (your Invoice (insert number), date __(maybe February__). We know our customers will be very pleased with them.

However, the spare parts and accessories that we ordered at the same time were not included. Was this an oversight, or are they being shipped later? We are enclosing a photocopy of our original order so that you can check this out quickly.

Please send these items to us by air parcel post, since we are anxious to complete our line.

Many thanks for your cooperation.

출처: Anderson et al.(1970), The Administrative Secretary, p.307 재구성

[수행순서] 반 ____ 학번 __________ 이름 __________ 제출일 __________

1. 다음 수행순서에 알맞게 문서가 작성되었는지 살펴보고 확인 칸에 체크표시하세요.

번호	수행순서	확인
1	문서의 수 · 발신 정보를 확인한다.	☐
2	영문서 서식을 정한다.	☐
3	선택한 서식파일을 연다.	☐
4	문서의 초안을 작성한다(문서의 내용을 확인한다).	☐
5	상사에게 보고하여 검토받는다.	☐
6	수정사항을 반영하여 완성한다. ★ 수정사항:	
		☐
		☐
		☐
		☐
		☐
		☐
		☐
		☐
		☐
		☐
7	상사의 결재를 받는다.	☐
8	수 · 발신 정보에 따라 발송한다.	☐

2. 본문의 내용을 아래에 해석하세요.

수행 15

홍성경 마케팅부문 전무는 비서에게 구조조정 관련 초안을 이메일로 보냈으니 확인을 해보고, 메모랜덤으로 작성해줄 것을 지시하였다. 그러면서 즉시 임원들(executive committee)에게 회람되도록 전자우편과 동시에 하드카피로도 배부되었으면 한다고 말씀하셨다.

홍 전무의 이메일을 확인한 비서는 바로 메모랜덤을 작성하여 상사에게 점검을 받았다. 이후 아래와 같은 상사의 피드백을 받았다. 피드백을 반영하여 영문서를 작성하세요.

MEMORANDUM

TO:	Executive Committee	FROM:	Sungkyung Hong
SUBJECT:	Reorganization of the Marketing Service Division	DATE:	11 August, 20–

Effectiv immediately, the marketing services division has been reorganized as follows. There will be four separate departments- customer services, market research, advertising, and field sales.

Jane Cliff is promoted to the position of Head of Customer Services, David Oh is promoted to Head of Market Research, Ethan Lee is promoted to Head of Advertising, and Min Hee Lim is promoted to Head of Field Sales.

The purpose of this new organizaiaton is to provide better guidance and supervision to the four area indicated and to place responsibility where it belongs.

Sungkyung Hong

출처: Poe and Fruehling(1989), Business Communication, McGraw Hill Book Company, p.322 재구성

문서 작성 Tip

≡: 대문자로
○sp: 철자확인
org. chart: 조직도 (* 새로 임명된 홍성경 전무는 마케팅 네 부서를 총괄 책임지는 마케팅부문 최고책임자이다)

조직도 예

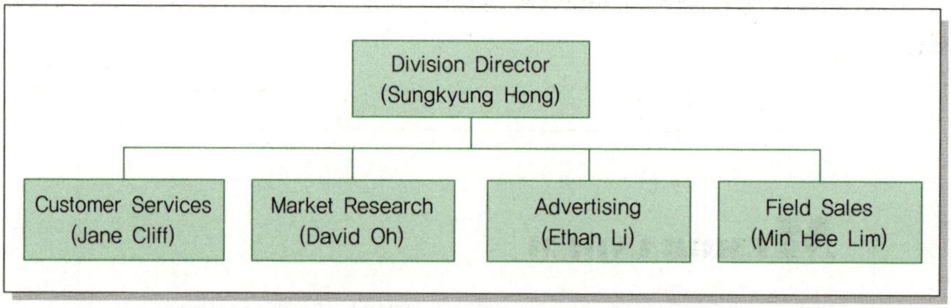

[수행순서] 반 ____ 학번 __________ 이름 __________ 제출일 __________

1. 다음 수행순서에 알맞게 문서가 작성되었는지 살펴보고 확인 칸에 체크표시하세요.

번호	수행순서	확인
1	문서의 수·발신 정보를 확인한다.	□
2	영문서 서식을 정한다.	□
3	선택한 서식파일을 연다.	□
4	문서의 초안을 작성한다(문서의 내용을 확인한다).	□
5	상사에게 보고하여 검토받는다.	□
6	수정사항을 반영하여 완성한다. ★ 수정사항:	
		□
		□
		□
		□
		□
		□
		□
		□
		□
		□
7	상사의 결재를 받는다.	□
8	수·발신 정보에 따라 발송한다.	□

2. 본문의 내용을 아래에 해석하세요.

Appendix

부 록

Appendix 1. 이력서(Resume)

구직자가 제출한 Cover Letter와 Resume는 인터뷰를 얻기 위한 중요한 수단이 된다. 그러므로 구직자는 독창적이며 적합한 자신만의 Resume를 작성하는 것이 중요하다.

1. 이력서 스타일

(1) 학력 중심의 Resume(Basic Resume)

학력 중심으로, 최근 순서대로 정리한 것이다. 갓 졸업자로서 처음 취직하는 경우나 경력이 적은 경우에 적절하다. 우리나라 이력서에 가장 가까운 형식이다. 학력 중심의 Resume는 한 장 이내에 두 장 이상 넘지 않도록 한다. 한 장 이내로 요약한다고 해도 너무 짧은 것은 내용이 빈약해 보여 좋은 Resume를 쓰겠다는 의욕이 부족하다고 여겨지게 되므로 지면을 요령 있게 사용토록 한다.

(2) 경력 중심의 Resume(Historical Resume)

경력 중심으로 최근 순서대로 역(逆) 연대순으로 정리한 것이다. 희망 직종에 관련있는 경력이나 업적 등을 차례대로 쓰는 형식으로, 경력이 많은 경우에 적당하다. 경력 중심의 Resume는 한 장이나 두 장이 적당하며, 희망하는 직종과 연관이 되고 지원하는 분야나 회사가 관심을 기울이는 것에 초점을 맞추어 쓰도록 한다. 경력은 최근 것이 중요하므로 최근 것부터 과거로 거슬러 올라가며 쓰되, 각 회사 내에서의 지위도 새로운 것부터 오래된 것의 순서대로 거슬러 올라가며 쓴다.

학력 중심의 이력서 스타일

(성명)
(주소)
(연락처)

OBJECTIVE (희망직종)

EDUCATION
Mar 20XX~Present (현재 또는 최근 학교명)
(학과명 혹은 전공분야)
Courses taken: (희망 직종에 관계 있는 주요과목)

Mar 20XX~Feb 20XX XX High School

WORK EXPERIENCE
(월/연도–월/연도) (희망 직종과 관련된 아르바이트 경험 포함)

ACTIVITIES
(월/연도–월/연도) (과외활동 : 동아리, 학생회활동 등)

CERTIFICATE
(취득한 월/연도) (검정 자격시험의 명칭, 등급, 발급기관)

SPECIAL SKILLS (워드프로세서, 타이핑 속도, 익숙한 OA기기
외국어능력 등)

REFERENCES (상황에 따라 이름, 주소, 전화번호를 쓰거나
References on request 등을 쓴다)

> **날짜를 쓸 때는:** 최근 것부터 쓴다. 학력, 경력, 수상 등.

> REFERENCES: 영문이력서에서는 대부분 추천인을 기재하도록 되어 있다. 당장 생각이 안 날 경우에는 '추후 제출(availabe upon request)'이라고 적는다.

Sample 1 대학 졸업예정자 학력 중심 이력서의 예(1)

SUMI KIM
122-8, Jangan4Dong, DongdaemunGu, Seoul (H) 02-789-1234 (C) 010-9500-1234
E-mail: sumi_kim@gmail.com

OBJECTIVE To obtain a secretary position which offers the opportunity for a career as an administrative assistant

EDUCATION

March 2017-Present Korea Women's University, Seoul
AA in Secretarial Administration (Expected in 2016)

- Courses taken:
  Secretarial Principles, Office Management, Business English, Economics, Business Law, Word-processing (in Korean and English), Filing System, Public Administration, Accounting Principles, etc.

March 2014-Feb. 2017 Korea High School, Seoul

CERTIFICATE

December 2017	Secretarial Skills Certificate, 2nd / 3 rd Grade, KCCI
July 2017	Certificate of Practical Legal Service Worker, KILE
September 2017	Korean Word Processing, 1st Grade, KCCI
May 2017	Practical Capability of Personal Computer, 2nd Grade, KCCI
March 2017	Hanja Ability 5thGrade, KCCI

ACTIVITIES

March 2017-Present Vice President
Member of KISC (Korea International Secretarial Club)
March 2017-Feb2017 Representative
Department of Secretarial Administration

SKILLS
English writing & speaking
Knowledge of all common office machines
Word Processing: Korean 600 ta, English 50wpm
Computer: Experienced in MS office, Photoshop, etc.

PERSONAL Communication skills, Accuracy in handling detail, A sense of responsibility, Cheerful personality

Sample 2 대학 졸업예정자 학력 중심 이력서의 예(2)

KIM, MI-KYUNG
3-216, Bukgajoa-Dong
Seadaemoon-Gu, Seoul 12013 (02) 305-1305 / Cell: 010-0299-349
e-mail: mk_kim@gmail.com

PERSONAL DATA
Born: January 28, 1994
Marital Status: Single
Health: Excellent

OBJECTIVE
Seeking for a position as a secretary

EDUCATION

Mar. 2016 ~ Feb. 2018	Secretarial Administration Dept. Kyung In Women's College, Inchon
Mar. 2013 ~ Feb. 2016	Myung-Ji Girl's High School , Seoul

Major Courses in College
Business English I, II
Practical Business Communication I, II
Secretarial Procedures I, II
Political Science
Business Management
Human Relations
Office Automation
Internet
Accounting

SKILLS
Secretarial Skills Certificate Examination 3rd Class, KCCI, 2017
Offical Examination-Word Processing Skills 2nd Class Written, KCCI, 2017
Offical Examination-Word Processing Skills 3rd Class, KCCI, 2017
Practical English Certificate Examination 4th grade 2017

Operating S/W packages: MS office, HWP, etc.

AWARDS & ACTIVITIES

2017	Scholarship for two years, Kyungin Women's College
2017 ~ Present	Acted as dept. representative
2017 ~ Aug.2017	Volunteer as an assistant of Town-Block Office
Nov. 2017	Volunteer as an assistant of Notrdam Nunnery

REFERENCES
Available on request.

경력 중심의 이력서 스타일

(성명)
(주소)
(연락처)

JOB OBJECTIVE	(희망직종)
QUALIFICATION	(희망직종에 관한 자격 요약)
WORK EXPERIENCE	
(월/연도–Present)	(현재 회사명, 도시명)
	(직위)
	(직책의 구체적 내용 혹은 업적)
(월/연도–월/연도)	(이전 회사명, 도시명)
	(직위)
	(직책의 구체적 내용 혹은 업적)
EDUCATION	
(월/연도–월/연도)	(최종 학교명)
	(학과명 내지 전공명)
ACTIVITIES	
(월/연도–월/연도)	(학창시절 과외활동의 특기사항, 업계 사회활동)
CERTIFICATE	
(취득한 월/연도)	(검정자격시험의 명칭, 등급, 발급기관)
REFERENCES	(상황에 따라 이름, 주소, 전화번호를 쓰거나 References on request 등을 쓴다)

Sample 3 대학 졸업예정자 경력 중심 이력서의 예

SUMI KIM

122-8, Jangan4Dong, DongdaemunGu, Seoul
(H) 02-789-1234 (C) 010-789-1234
E-mail: sumi_kim@gmail.com

OBJECTIVE — *To obtain a secretary position which offers the opportunity for a career as an administrative assistant*

EDUCATION

March 2016 - Present — Korea Women's University, Seoul
AA in Secretarial Administration (Expected in 2018)

WORK EXPERIENCE

Mar 2017 –Jun2017 — AMERICA CORPORATION..Chicago
Assistant to Sales Manager (Internship)

- *Responsibilities:* Writing letters and reports, word processing using Excel and PowerPoint, etc.

Mar 2016–Nov2016 — SAMSUNG SECURITIES CO., LTD.....................................Seoul
Team Secretary to Human Resources Team

- *Responsibilities*: General secretarial activities, such as greeting callers, receiving calls, writing routine letters and reports, etc.

CERTIFICATES & SKILLS

December 2017 — Secretarial Skills Certificate Examination 2nd Grade, KCCI
July 2017 — Official TOEIC Score: 900, ETS
December 2016 — Korean Word Processing, 1st Grade, KCCI
December 2016 — Driving license 2nd Grade, KoROAD

- Writing & Speaking in English(Advanced)
- Have working knowledge of all common office machines
- Computer: Excel, PowerPoint, PhotoShop, etc.

ACTIVITIES & AWARDS

Jan2017–Feb2017 — Study abroad for language learning at Hawaii University
Mar2016–Jun2016 — Volunteer work at Academy of HRD
March 2016 — Scholarship for two years, Korea Women's University

References available upon request

Appendix 2. 비서관련 교과목 영문표기

비서관련 교과목 영문표기를 숙지하고 있으면 영문이력서 작성이나 영어 면접 시 활용할 수 있으므로 반드시 숙지하도록 한다.

• 비서학 개론	Secretarial Principles
• 사무행정업무관리	Office Administration Management
• 비즈니스영문서관리	Managing Business Documents
• 비즈니스영어회화	Business English Conversation
• 문서작성 · 관리	Document Writing & Management
• 비즈니스컴퓨팅	Business Computing
• 데이터관리	Data Management
• 전산회계실무	Practical Electronic Accounting
• 경영환경동향분석	Principles to Business Administration
• 대인업무관리	Using the Phone & Receiving Visitors
• 일정 · 출장관리	Schedule Management
• 회의 · 의전관리	Conference Management
• 경영진지원업무	Management Support Services
• 필수과목	Required Subjects
• 선택과목	Elective Subjects
• 교양과목	Liberal Subjects

Appendix 3. 미국의 주 이름과 약어

우리나라 우편번호에 해당되는 것이 미국의 Zip Code이다. 이 경우 미국의 주는 대문자 약어로 표시가 되는 것이 대부분이다. 봉투에 표시된 약어를 보고 어느 주를 뜻하는 것인지를 알 수 있도록 익히도록 한다.

[STATES]

Alabama	AL	Kentucky	KY	Oklahoma	OK
Alaska	AK	Louisiana	LA	Oregon	OR
American Samoa	AS	Maine	ME	Pennsylvania	PA
Arizona	AZ	Maryland	MD	Puerto Rico	PR
Arkansas	AR	Massachusetts	MA	Rhode Island	RI
California	CA	Michigan	MI	South Carolina	SC
Canal Zone	CZ	Minnesota	MN	South Dakota	SD
Colorado	CO	Mississippi	MS	Tennessee	TN
Connecticut	CT	Missouri	MO	Texas	TX
Delaware	DE	Montana	MT	Trust Territories	TT
District of Columbia	DC	Nebraska	NE	Utah	UT
Florida	FL	Nevada	NV	Vermont	VT
Georgia	GA	New Hampshire	NH	Virginia	VA
Guam	GU	New Jersey	NJ	Virgin Islands	VI
Hawaii	HI	New Mexico	NM	Washington	WA
Idaho	ID	New York	NY	West Virginia	WV
Illinois	IL	North Carolina	NC	Wisconsin	WI
Indiana	IN	North Dakota	ND	Wyoming	WY
Iowa	IA	Northern Mariana Is.	CM		
Kansas	KS	Ohio	OH		

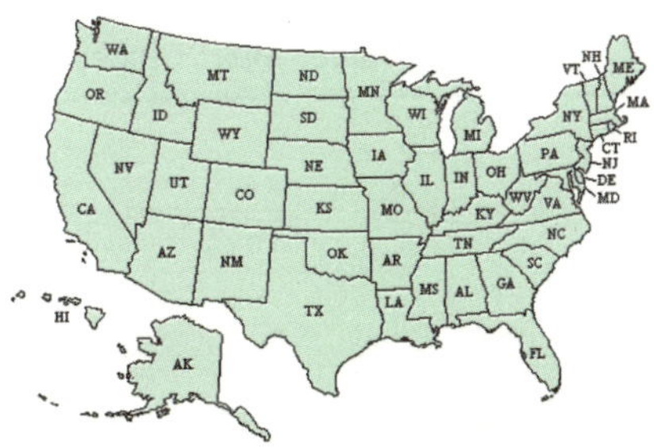

Appendix 4. 부서명 및 직함명

비서는 최소한 자기 회사의 부서명과 직함명은 영어로 숙지하고 있어야 한다. 직함명과 부서명은 회사마다 표기방식이 다소 다를 수 있으므로 자신의 회사에서 사용되는 영문표기 방식을 알아두어야 한다.

[부서명]

사장실	CEO Office/ President Office
비서실	Secretarial Department
~ 국	~ Bureau
~ 부	~ Division, Department
~ 과	~ Section
~ 팀	~ Team
총무부	General Affairs Department, Administrative Div.
재무부	Finance Dept.
경리부	Accounting Dept.
인사부	Human Resources / Personnel Dept.
기획조정실	Planning & Coordination Dept.
영업부	Sales Dept.
구매부	Purchasing Dept.
마케팅부	Marketing Dept.
제조부	Production Dept.
홍보부	Public Relations Dept., Public Affairs Dept.
연구개발부	Research & Development Dept.
전산실	Information Technology Dept.
지점	Branch Office
본사	Head Office, Main Office, Headquarters

[직함명]

회장	Chairperson
부회장	Vice Chairperson
사장	President, President and Representative Director
부사장	Vice President, Executive Vice President
대표이사	Representative Director
최고경영책임자	Chief Executive Officer: CEO
최고재무책임자	Chief Financial Officer: CFO
최고운영책임자	Chief Operating Officer: COO
최고기술책임자	Chief Technology Officer: CTO
최고서비스총괄책임자	Chief Product Officer: CPO
최고마케팅책임자	Chief Marketing Officer: CMO
전무이사	Senior Managing Director
상무이사	Executive Director, Managing Director
이사	Director
(상임) 감사	(Standing) Auditor
고문	Advisor
부장	General Manager
영업부장	Sales Manager
총무부장	General Affairs Manager
팀장	Team Manager
부장	Senior Manager
과장/차장	Manager
경리부장	Accounting Manager
대리	Assistant Manager
감독자	Superintendent, Supervisor
지점장	Branch Manager
지사장/총지배인(호텔)	General Manager
비서	Secretary, Office Administrative Assistant
전문비서	Executive Secretary / Office Professional Administrative Professional
안내직원	Receptionist

Appendix 5. 사무기기 및 사무용품 용어

[사무기기 및 사무용품 명칭]

- 복사기: photocopier, copier
- 팩스: fax machine, facsimile
- 편지개봉 칼: paper knife
- 계산기: calculator
- 클립: paper clip
- 제침기: remover
- 자: ruler
- 풀: glue
- 흰색칠판: white board
- 파일박스: file box, file cabinet
- 고무밴드: rubber band
- 연필깎기: pencil sharpener
- 호치키스: stapler
- 펀치: punch
- 지우개: eraser
- 가위: scissors
- 칸막이: partition
- 수신용 서류함: in-box
- 미처리 서류함: hold-box
- 발송용 서류함: out-box

[꼭 암기하세요!]

- 전표: slip
- 전화메모: telephone message
- 청구서: bill
- 구매주문서: purchase order
- 메모: memo(memorandum의 약어)
- 통지: notice
- 견적서: estimate
- 서류: document, paper, correspondence
- 보고서: report
- 송장: invoice
- 재고표: inventory list
- 가격표: price list
- 영수증: receipt
- 급여명세서: pay slip

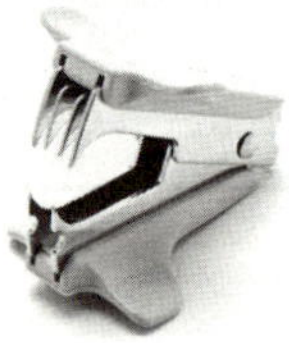

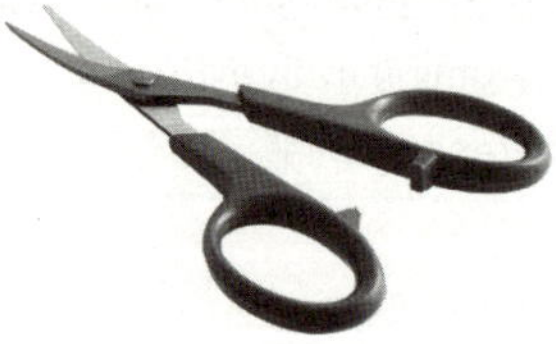

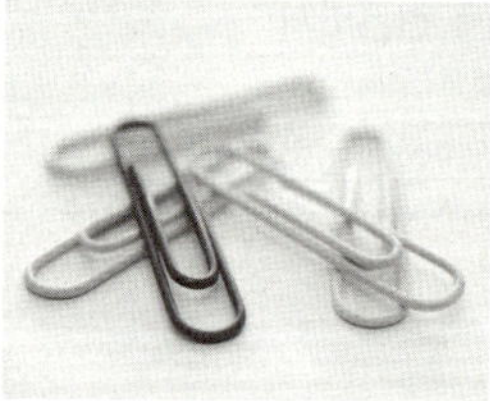

| 저자소개 |

■ 민선향

현) 배화여자대학교 비서행정과 교수
연세대학교 대학원 교육학 박사
미국 Virginia Polytechnic Institute & State University 박사연구과정 1년
미국 University of Pittsburgh 교육학 석사
이화여자대학교 비서학과 학사

■ 박경옥

현) 이화여자대학교 국제사무학과 초빙교수
영국 University of Birmingham 경영학 박사
연세대학교 국제학대학원 국제경영학 석사
이화여자대학교 비서학과 학사

■ 유근선

현) 인덕대학교 비서학과 교수
영국 University of St Andrews, School of Management 방문연구원
고려대학교 국제대학원 국제통상학 박사
이화여자대학교 대학원 비서학 석사
이화여자대학교 비서학과 학사

■ 장은주

현) 경인여자대학교 비서행정과 교수
미국 Syracuse University, Whitman School of Management 교환교수
서강대학교 대학원 경영학 박사
서강대학교 경영대학원 경영학 석사
이화여자대학교 비서학과 학사

■ 하선영

현) 이화여자대학교 국제사무학과 외래교수
숭실대학교 대학원 교육학 박사
이화여자대학교 대학원 비서학 석사
이화여자대학교 비서학과 학사

NCS 기반 **비즈니스 영문서 핸드북**

2017년 9월 5일 1판 1쇄 발행
2021년 8월 25일 1판 3쇄 발행

저 자 | 민선향 · 장은주 · 박경옥 · 하선영 · 유근선
발 행 인 | 이수영
발 행 처 | 도서출판 청람
서울시 마포구 독막로 288(대흥동, 세양상가 109호)
전 화 | 02) 3272-2601~2
팩 스 | 02) 3272-2603
이 메 일 | crbooks@daum.net
홈페이지 | http://www.crbooks.co.kr
등 록 | 2000년 8월 26일 제6-0509호

ISBN 978-89-5972-598-4 93320 [정가 18,000원]